Life In An Elevator

This book is dedicated to my Mom, Elaine,
who, as one of my blog reader's put it,
is a real trip.
Thanks, Mom, for always
being there for me.

Life In An Elevator

Table of Contents

TV TIME   1

BREAKFAST WITH DREW	2
SOAP ON A ROPE	3
METEOROLOGY 101	4
PACK YOUR BAG	5
ARIZONA TIME ZONE WARP	6
WHEEL OF PRICE IS RIGHT	8
BRAIN DEAD	9
REPEAT OFFENDER	10
PENGUIN WALK-ABOUT	11
TENNIS ANYONE?	12
COUNTING SHEEP INSTEAD OF CALORIES	13
PENGUIN WALK-ABOUT - THE SEQUEL	15
OLE	16
EAR OF THE BEHOLDER	17
RACK 'EM UP	18

CURRENT EVENTS   19

A DOOBIE A DAY KEEPS THE DOCTOR AWAY	20
OVER WHERE?	21
SEX IN THE SUN CITY	22
TURN RIGHT, TURN RIGHT... OH, NEVER MIND	23
HAPPY BIRTHDAY MR. WALLACE	24
BATTER UP	25
GRUMPY GUY	26
MERCURY RUN AMOK	27
THREE STOOGES	28
BOOBY TRAP	29
SHERIFF JOE FOR PRESIDENT?	30
MURDER'S AFOOT	31

Life In An Elevator

ON THE HOME FRONT	**32**
MY MOM WON'T LET ME GET A PUPPY	33
HAIRDRESSER MATH	35
THE SLIMFAST MYSTERY	36
LIFE IN AN ELEVATOR	37
PUBLISHER'S CLEARINGHOUSE AND OTHER GAMES OF CHANCE	38
THE PHONE BOOKS COMETH	40
LAST WOMAN STANDING	41
THE MAGICAL FRUIT	42
MEAN, GREEN ICE CREAM MACHINE	44
HELP I'VE FALLEN AND I CAN'T STOP TALKING ABOUT IT	46
SUN CITY LOCK DOWN	48
I HEAR VOICES	50
MARTHA STEWART HAS LEFT THE BUILDING	52
PATTY'S TATTIE	54
TIME OUTS FOR EVERYONE!	55
THE BOBBERS	**56**
THE BOBBERS	57
THE MAD HATTER	59
SUN CITY TRIVIA	61
TUMMY TUCKS ARE FOR SISSIES	63
MEMORIES - GOING, GOING, GONE	65
WASTE MANAGEMENT	**67**
TO SOFTEN OR NOT TO SOFTEN	68
ONE IF BY PEE	69
THE SOFTENING SAGA - PART 2	70
MEXICAN BEANS	71
THE SOFTENING SAGA - PART 3	72

Life In An Elevator

FRIENDS AND FAMILY — 73
- LIFE LESSON #19 — 74
- DON'T YOU JUST HATE THOSE X-RATED CONDOS? — 75
- TAKE MY MONEY, PLEASE — 76
- MR. WINKY — 77
- BITE ME? — 78
- SINK OR SWIM — 79

I'M JUST SAYING — 81
- MOM-ISIMS — 82
- I'LL TAKE THINGY'S FOR $20, ALEX... — 83
- DINING OUT MEANS EATING IN — 85
- BRIGHT LIGHTS AND OTHER NIGHT TIME FUN — 86
- OLD COWBOYS NEVER DIE - THEY JUST GET DE-RANGED — 87
- SKATING ON THIN ICE — 88
- WHAT?!? — 89
- THE END OF THE WORLD — 90
- MYSTERY CHUNK — 91
- THE SAMSON EFFECT — 92
- CHINESE TACOS — 93
- HOW TO BE ARTLESS IN ARIZONA — 94
- DOGGONE — 95
- CURFEW — 96
- THE RAPUNZEL PHOBIA — 98
- ALERT THE MEDIA — 99
- THE REAL SKINNY — 100
- NO GOATS ALLOWED — 101

Life In An Elevator

NEIGHBORS AND OTHER LOCAL WILDLIFE — 102
- ESTATE SALES R US — 103
- NEIGHBORHOOD WATCH — 104
- THE ARIZONA HYENA OUTBREAK — 105
- OMG - JESUS SAW ME NAKED! — 106
- TALIBAN RABBITS — 107
- WILEY COYOTES — 108
- POINT, CLICK, ARRRRG — 109
- THE TARANTULA IN THE DRYER — 110
- NOT WOLVERINES — 113
- LOVEY DOVEY — 114
- BUGS BUNNY MEETS BILLY THE KID — 115
- A SUN CITY ROOFIE — 117
- LOOPY — 118
- THE QUAIL SPA — 119
- A GRENADE IN THE HAND IS WORTH TWO IN THE CLOSET — 120

OUT AND ABOUT — 121
- IN THE BAG — 122
- A YARN ABOUT YARN — 123
- SWIMMING WITH SHARKS — 125
- PARKING LOT GAMES — 127
- RUNAWAY WALKER — 128
- THE TEQUILA WAGON — 130
- THE GREAT STRAWBERRY WAR — 131
- BEACH ANGELS AND STUD MUFFINS — 132
- GOD'S RECEPTION AREA — 133

Life In An Elevator

Life In An Elevator

TV Time

Life In An Elevator

BREAKFAST WITH DREW

Life with Mom involves rituals. During the week, dinner is eaten in the living room watching the 6:00 news, followed by Wheel of Fortune. Breakfast happens at the kitchen table doing the Arizona Republic crosswords while consuming 10 ounces of OJ, coffee, a banana and a granola breakfast bar. Sometimes we are able to intersperse the meal routine with a slice of homemade zucchini bread or half a grapefruit. There's a small TV in the kitchen so breakfast is *always* accompanied by Drew Carey and The Price is Right at 9:00.

Every couple of weeks or so I'm summoned to the kitchen during The Price Is Right, usually with Mom frantically shouting "Patty, you've got to see this!"

As I walk toward the kitchen table, I'm greeted with a variation of the following dialog.

"Just look at this. This woman has the biggest boobs I've ever seen. Now watch, watch. She'll start to jump up and down and I'll bet she doesn't even have a bra on."

"But Mom, I thought jumping up and down was a prerequisite to being on The Price Is Right."

"Maybe, but it shouldn't be if your boobs are so big they could knock out the host."

Life In An Elevator

SOAP ON A ROPE

While eating dinner in front of the TV shortly after the new year, a news story about a recently released felon who was involved in a shooting inside the Chandler Mall had just finished up and the newsperson announced that, since afternoon programming had been interrupted to cover the story earlier in the day, the daytime soap, General Hospital, would be rerun a 1:40 a.m.

"I guess people can't miss their soaps," I laughed.

"Nope, I guess not," my husband Bill responded.

"I know, I heard that earlier," Mom interjected. "They're going to show the story again between 1 and 2 o'clock in hospitals."

"No, Mom," I said, "They're going to replay the soap opera."

"No," she insisted. "They said they were going to show the story again because people in hospitals didn't get to see it."

"No, they're going to replay the program 'General Hospital' at 1:40 in the morning - not repeat the news story in hospitals between 1 and 2 in the morning!" Bill explained.

"Oh, well, that makes more sense then what they said before." she replied.

Life In An Elevator

METEOROLOGY 101

Watching the weather report on the evening news, the weather map showed rain in a line, north and south, from Flagstaff to Tucson, but nothing in Phoenix.

"Look at that, Mom, it's raining north of us and south of us. Why can't we get some rain here in the middle where we are?"

"Because the rain comes from the west!" she explained, as though that should make perfect sense.

Life In An Elevator

PACK YOUR BAG

I was bringing Mom's dinner plate to her while we all sat in the living room watching the local evening news.

"Did you hear about that man that tried to break out of jail?" she asked during a commercial break.

"Nope," I replied. "Was it here?"

"I don't think so. I think it was in Mexico. Anyway, his girlfriend tried to get him out in a suitcase."

"She must have been pretty hefty to carry out a full grown man in a suitcase."

"Maybe it was a roller bag," Bill commented.

"Maybe so," I said.

"But they caught him because he was in feces," Mom added, grinning from ear to ear.

"WHAT," Bill and I exclaimed together.

"That's what they said on the story."

"They said he was in a suitcase full of poop?"

"Yup - he was caught laying in feces positions."

"Do you mean fetal position?" I asked, trying hard not to laugh.

"Oh, maybe. But that's still how they caught him. That and the fact that the woman was sweating and dragging the bag and acting nervous."

"Plus she probably pooped her pants too," Bill sputtered, trying not to choke on his Subway.

Life In An Elevator

ARIZONA TIME ZONE WARP

In the last few months, Mom, along with millions of other people, have rediscovered Betty White. I think Mom feels a connection with Ms. White because of the closeness of their age. Every time she sees Betty White on a talk show or in a commercial, it jogs her memory that she's in a sitcom - she just can't remember the name of it, when it's on, or what station is carrying it. So - without fail, whenever she see Betty White on TV - whether it's on a talk show or in a commercial - she'll call me into the room. And, as soon as I see what's on the screen, I'll blurt out "Hot In Cleveland. Wednesday. 7 o'clock.. TV Land." At this point, she'll grab the TV magazine that comes with the Sunday paper and double check in case I'm wrong.

Unfortunately, the local TV magazines lists the start times for all the satellite/cable channels in Eastern Daylight Time - not in Arizona-Mountain-We-Never-Go-On-Daylight-Savings-Time, which means that everything is listed as starting three hours before it actually comes on the air. Hot In Cleveland is listed on TVL as beginning at 4:00 not 7:00. This is frustrating, but Mom has been able to compensate, for the most part, by only watching local channels or memorizing when her favorite satellite shows are on. Something new, like Hot In Cleveland, throws a monkey-wrench into her TV watching system. And, for reasons that are beyond my ability to comprehend, she refuses to use the on-screen Direct TV Guide. Maybe pushing the ON/OFF button and number buttons represent the limit of her technical capabilities because at least once a week there's a TV crisis that results in her yelling for Bill. The problem is always a result of her pushing the wrong buttons on the remote and creating a 'No Signal' or a snowy screen.

This past Sunday night as I passed through the living room around 7:30, I noticed she had a 'newsertainment' program on - it was 20/20 or 60 minutes or Dateline. I'm not sure which because they all look the same to me.

"You know Mom, Hot In Cleveland is on TV Land right now."

"No it isn't. It's on Wednesday."

"I know, but TV Land is showing some of the old episodes so you can catch up if you want."

As usual, she grabbed the TV magazine to verify the information before tuning in to channel 304. She flipped pages back and forth for a minute before looking up at me. "Well I can't watch it now. It was on three hours ago."

"No, that's just the way the TV guide lists them, remember?"

"Oh, right. But I still can't watch it now."

"Why?" I asked, since I knew it was a multi-episode marathon.

Life In An Elevator

"Because the TV guide says it started at 5:00 and it almost 8:00 now so it ended an hour ago!"

I chose not to argue with her illogic this time and instead I left the room without further comment, seriously debating a pre-bedtime cocktail. After all, according to the TV magazine, it's 5:00 somewhere!

Life In An Elevator

WHEEL OF PRICE IS RIGHT

I think Mom has invented her own game show. I'm not sure what the rules are, but she seemed to have come up with it in between bites of cashew chicken. We were eating dinner and watching the local 6:00 news when they played a promotion for Wheel of Fortune, which follows the news at 6:30. "That's Jodie," she exclaimed suddenly. "She really won big last night."

"She must have," I commented. "It shows her winning $30,000. She must have done all right on the final puzzle."

"She did and it was lucky she even got it, but she hit one dollar exactly."

"One dollar?" I asked.

"Yes, you know. Two people spin and the closest one to the real price gets to bid."

"Mom, that's Price Is Right. This was Wheel of Fortune."

"No, it's Wheel of Fortune. You and another person spins the wheel and the closest to a dollar gets to solve the final puzzle."

"Did they change the rules?"

"Well they must have because Jodie won now, didn't she."

Life In An Elevator

BRAIN DEAD

While watching the Oscar buzz on TV the morning before the awards show, Bill and I were discussing how unoriginal the movies had become - instead taking themes from fairy tales and comic books.

"The only original ideas seemed to be movies that are made using computer-generated animation." I commented.

Mom broke into the conversation. "You know what the problem is," she said, trying to sound wise. "People are spending all their time talking on their cell phones or sitting behind computers and that's why they can't think of any new movie ideas."

Life In An Elevator

REPEAT OFFENDER

Before going to bed one night, Mom poked her head into the family room to say good night. "I sure hope the new TV shows are better than the ones now" she commented.

"You mean the new fall shows."

"Yes. The stuff this season is terrible."

I was confused, since this was a Tuesday and her three favorite shows were on. "Mom, I thought you liked The Good Wife."

"No, I don't. They just keep working on these cases."

"But it's a show about lawyers," I explained. "Lawyers work on cases."

"I don't know about that. I just know it's stupid."

"You didn't think it was stupid when you watched the first runs. Why are the repeats stupid."

"Because they're showing the same thing over again instead of coming up with new ideas."

Life In An Elevator

PENGUIN WALK-ABOUT

"Did you hear about the penguins?" Mom asked as I was making my way through the living room into the kitchen.

"Penguin? What penguin?" I said.

"The one that swam here," she replied. "It was on the news."

"Swam from where?"

"From New Zealand."

"And it swam here? To Arizona?"

"No, not here-here. Somewhere else here."

"You mean like California or Oregon?"

"Yes, someplace like that. I don't remember where exactly. Anyway, they're raising money."

"They?" I asked, becoming even more confused. "Who's they?"

"The people where the penguin swam to."

"Raising money for what? To give to the penguin?"

"No, to send it back to New Zealand."

"Mom, they don't have penguins in New Zealand. How could it come from New Zealand?"

"I don't know, but that's what they said."

I left the room, shaking my head and continued my trek into the kitchen where I found Bill with his hands over his mouth, tears streaming down his face, laughing so hard he was doubled over.

"OK, smarty," I whispered. "What's the real story?"

Trying to pull himself together, he sputtered "Antarctica. To New Zealand. Not California."

Life In An Elevator

TENNIS ANYONE?

While we were eating dinner the other night, the local news had a teaser about an upcoming Wimbledon story for the sports segment of the broadcast.

"I wonder where they play that now?" Mom said.

"Play what? Wimbledon?" I asked, somewhat confused.

"Yes, I wonder where they have it nowadays."

"At Wimbledon in England," I replied. "Just like they always do. Why, where else do you think it would be?"

"Oh, I don't know. I didn't know if they moved it someplace else for a change."

"Then I guess it wouldn't be called Wimbledon anymore," Bill piped in.

"I don't know about that. They still call it the Daytona 400 but it's somewhere else."

"It is?" Bill said.

"Where?" I asked.

"I'm not sure, but I know they moved it from Indiana to another place - somewhere around Illinois. Or maybe New Mexico."

Life In An Elevator

COUNTING SHEEP INSTEAD OF CALORIES

"Patty!" came the call from the living room as I was trying to get dinner ready before the 6:00 deadline. I walked in and stood in front of Mom, who was playing her little electronic poker game.

"What's up?" I asked.

"There's going to be a story on the news but I forget what it's about."

"Well, enjoy the news," I said as I started walking away.

"No, wait," she called after me. "It was something I wanted you to see."

"Okay. Then let me know when it comes on," I answered, making my way back into the kitchen. A few moments later, she called to me again.

"Patty, it's on."

I walked back into the living room where the story was about a suspected suicide in California. "Is this the story you wanted me to see?" I asked.

"No. I just wanted you to know the news is back on."

"Do you remember the story yet?"

"No, but I'll know it when I see it," she said. "I'll be sure to let you know."

"Okey, dokey," I replied, returning once again to the kitchen.

A few minutes later, she yelled again. "Patty, it's coming on."

Returning to the living room one more time, the TV greeted me with a cell phone commercial. "Mom, this isn't the news."

"I know, but it's coming on right after this."

We both watched a fast food restaurant commercial.

"Okay, right after this," she promised.

"What's this story about?" I asked as an insurance commercial started.

"I can't remember, but it'll be coming up next."

And sure enough, right after we finished watching the Good Hands people, followed by a healthy dental check-up because of mouthwash-laden toothpaste, the local news returned.

"Here it is," she exclaimed, clearly excited about the upcoming report.

The news anchor offered a tease about losing weight in your sleep, followed by a study that showed after vigorous exercise, people - particularly men - continued to lose calories for as long as 14 hours.

"That's the story?" I asked. "If we exercise really hard, we'll burn calories in our sleep?"

Life In An Elevator

"Well that's not right," Mom grumbled. "I thought they'd tell me how to lose weight in bed by taking a pill or something, not by working out. I'm too old to work out!"

"I'm guessing the last time you did anything close to resembling exercise I probably hadn't reached puberty yet," I muttered over my shoulder as I marched back into the kitchen to help Bill, who was frying up a non-diet fish and chips dinner.

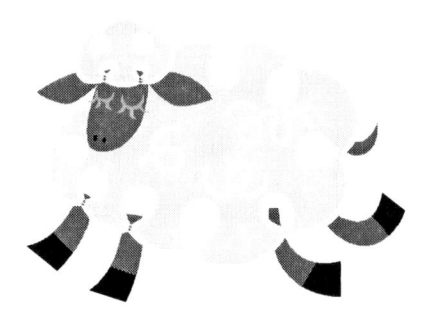

Life In An Elevator

PENGUIN WALK-ABOUT - THE SEQUEL

Several months ago there was a story on the news about an Emperor Penguin that got lost and ended up swimming from Antarctica to New Zealand. He became critically ill from eating sand, which he seems to have mistook for snow. The follow-up story was about the penguin's remarkable recovery and how he was being returned to his home in a special snow-filled glass cage aboard an Antarctica-bound research vessel.

At the time of the original event, I got a convoluted version of the story from Mom (see Penguin Walk-About) but, since we were all sitting in front of the TV watching the same news story on the penguins recovery and upcoming return to Antarctica, I assumed she'd have an accurate grasp on this follow-up event. Wrong!

"Isn't that nice," she said when the story ended. "I guess they raised enough money to send him back to New Zealand."

"Who sent him where?" Bill stuttered, looking towards me as I sat on the couch munching my pizza and preparing to take mental blog notes.

"California," she said. "I remember when that penguin landed there and they were going to raise money to send him back."

"Back to New Zealand?" Bill asked. "He's from Antarctica, not New Zealand."

"Well then why are they sending him back to New Zealand?" Mom asked.

"They aren't, Mom," Bill answered, closing his eyes and slowly shaking his head. I could read his mind and he was thinking 'why didn't I just shut up!' "They're sending him back to Antarctica."

"Well that's just crazy. If the boat trip from California doesn't kill him, then getting dumped on a strange iceberg will!"

I think Bill almost lost an eye because they were both bulging out of his face, which was also turning a lovely ripe tomato red. His glasses seemed to steam up, and could be what caused him to bump into the door frame as he escaped into the kitchen.

15

Life In An Elevator

OLE

It's the Fall Premier Season on TV and Bill and I were watching one of our favorites, *Fringe*. During a commercial break, I needed to take my own break and wandered through the living room on my way to the bathroom. I was stopped dead in my tracks by what Mom seemed to be watching on the TV.

"Mom," I said gently, "What in the world do you have on?"

"It's the Family."

"Do you mean Family Feud?"

"No, the Family channel. It's supposed to be Funniest Home Videos."

"But they're speaking Spanish," I commented.

"That's just a commercial," she responded.

"Okay, but that sounds like Spanish too," I said as the next advertisement began.

"Well, it's probably only the commercials then," she rationalized.

"What channel number is this?" I asked.

"I think it's 39."

"I hate to burst your bubble, Mom, but that's a Spanish-speaking station."

"It is?" she asked, then picked up the TV Guide to double-check. "Why would they show Funniest Home Videos," she muttered, leafing through the pages of the Guide. "That's an American show."

I left her pouring over her beloved TV Guide and counter-checking it with the local newspaper's version, the TV Magazine. If nothing else, Mom is a thorough researcher of all things related to television programming. Plus, I figured that would keep her busy until *Blue Bloods* came on. She has that channel number memorized.

Life In An Elevator

EAR OF THE BEHOLDER

Quite often, when Mom sees a news story on TV or reads it in the paper, she only hears part of it or her interpretation of it is somewhat eschewed. For example, a while back during dinner time, a news story teaser came on just before a commercial break, hinting at a problem with children not receiving immunizations in Europe because of an Autism scare.

"They had this story on before and there's a problem because a doctor told parents that if kids with Autism are vaccinated, it could kill them,' Mom commented. "So the parents didn't get them their shots and now the kids are dying from the diseases."

"That's nuts," I replied. "Why would a vaccine be any different for a child with Autism. It's not like an allergy."

"I don't know, but that's what they said."

When the story played a few minutes later and explained the study conducted in Europe, it showed that, for some children, if they were given a "cocktail" vaccine, it might <u>cause</u> Autism.

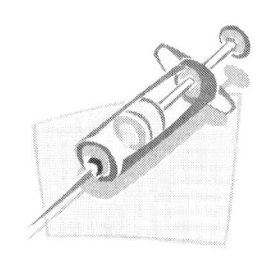

Life In An Elevator

RACK 'EM UP

There's a commercial on TV that shows a bright, precocious little girl maturing through childhood, then on a game show as a pre-teen, running for office in high school and finally graduating from college to become a pharmacist. The producer did a remarkable job of matching the looks of each of the four actress, although Mom was under the impression that it was all the same person.

"I sure would like to know how they managed to make that girl look bigger," she commented.

"They use an actress for each of her ages," I explained.

"Well, that commercial would sure take a long time to make," she exclaimed.

"No, Mom, they don't film the same person as she ages, they hire actresses that all look similar."

"I don't know about that," she said. "It looks like the same person to me only stretched out."

I could hear Bill in the kitchen, snickering and mumbling something about those crazy Hollywood people using the rack to stretch harmless children for commercials..

Current Events

Life In An Elevator

A DOOBIE A DAY KEEPS THE DOCTOR AWAY

Medical Marijuana continues to be a front and center story here in Arizona and Mom has her opinions on the subject. We've pretty much ignored her 'sky is falling' comments until we noticed a story in the Sun City newspaper indicating the delay in implementing it would affect many seniors and cause a lot of problems. Even though the voters passed the bill, our governor has put implementation on hold until she's sure no federal laws would be broken since the Obama administration seems to continue to single out Arizona for legal scrutiny. This is in direct contrast to our neighboring state of Californication, where doctor's offices are set up on each side of a dispensary and prescriptions are given out for medical pot like they were passing out granola bar samples at Costco - with no federal intervention.

But I digress... Watching the news one night, Mom said how putting this on hold would be bad because it would force people to get their weed illegally. Bill and I looked at each other and telegraphed "isn't that how they do it now?" with our eyes.

"It seems to be causing a lot of problems in Sun City," Bill commented after the story on TV ended. "Seniors claim they won't be able to get their pot."

"I know, it's awful. Now they'll have to suffer needlessly" Mom lamented.

Mom's level of concern confused us further because it was coming from the same person that thought legalization was the worst thing that could happen to the state and that Arizonans would all burn in hell (as if we don't in the summer anyway!) if it was legalized.

"Mom, nobody's suffering. They have ways of getting their marijuana if they need it," I said.

Ignoring me, she continued... "They'll be forced to grow it in their backyards, or order it from the black market. It's just a mess"

"Mom, it's not a mail-order business," Bill commented.

"I don't know about that but this medical marijuana thing is really going to cause problems, I just know it is. It's going to be big trouble."

And that starts with a T and rhymes with a P and that stands for POT!

Life In An Elevator

OVER WHERE?

Walking into the kitchen for a coffee refill this morning, Mom commented "I hope they leave soon."

I glanced at the TV and she had on the local morning news on Fox. They were showing footage of Mexican troops and doing a story on the drug cartels.

"What do you mean leave?" I asked. "Leave where?"

"There," she relied, nodding towards the TV screen.

"You mean Mexico?"

"No, I mean there."

"Where?"

"You know, that place over there where we're fighting."

"Do you mean Afghanistan?"

"Yes. They should leave."

"But Mom," I explained. "The news story is about drug cartels in Mexico."

"Then what on earth are our troops doing in Mexico?"

"They're not - those are Mexican soldiers and Mexican police."

"Oh. Well, they should get them out of there too."

"Get who out of where?"

"Those drug people. They should get them out."

"Well, I think they're trying," I responded.

"Then they better snap it up because it's only going to get worse with this medical marijuana thing!"

I fled the room, vowing never to return.

21

Life In An Elevator

SEX IN THE SUN CITY

Who would have thought that Sun City was a hot spot for rampant sex? Well, according to the local Sun City paper, there's a problem here with seniors contracting STDs. This fact was made known to Bill and me over dinner the other night.

"You know," Mom said during a Wheel of Fortune commercial break, "this SDS here is pretty bad."

Bill and I looked at each other in confusion. "SDS?" Bill asked.

"Yes, that's what the paper called it. It stands for Sex Diseases something or something."

"OK," I bit. "How about Sex Diseases in Seniors? Or Seniors Doing Sex?"

"No, it was something else," she continued, not at all phased by my attempt at humor. "All these old farts are running around have sex with each other and passing diseases back and forth."

"What kind of diseases?" Bill asked, winking at me.

"Oh, you know, sex diseases. Like shingles and lice."

"Lice?" Bill and I said together.

"Yes, you know, those bugs that people get in their privates."

"Do you mean crabs?" I asked.

"OK, those too I guess," she said. "But if they'd just stop for awhile, the diseases would probably run their course and go away. But they don't. They just keep fooling around like they were kids. It's ridiculous!"

Life In An Elevator

TURN RIGHT, TURN RIGHT... OH, NEVER MIND

"Did you see the news story about making traffic better?" Mom asked one evening.

"Nope," I responded. "What story?"

"Well, they did a study and they found that if people just made right turns, it would really help traffic move better and there would be less accidents. So now they're trying it out in some town somewhere. And if you have to go left, you either turn with the flow of traffic or you go farther up the street and turn around in one of those boulevard cut outs, then go back and make a right."

"Do you mean islands?" I asked.

"No, here in Phoenix," she answered. "What difference would it make how people drove on an island? They can't go far any way because of the water."

"I think they were talking about traffic circles, Mom," Bill interjected.

"No, they were talking about making right turns to avoid left turns. Not driving around in circles. That would be crazy!"

Life In An Elevator

HAPPY BIRTHDAY MR. WALLACE

"The paper says Mike Wallace is 93 today" Mom commented one morning before she started in on the crossword.

"Wow," I said. "That's amazing. I think he's still doing stuff on 60 Minutes."

"Oh no, he does the Fox Sunday morning program."

"Mom," I responded with a silent sigh. "That's his son, Chris."

"Oh, then I guess he doesn't look as good as I thought," she replied.

Life In An Elevator

BATTER UP

Watching a cable news channel, a reporter was giving an update on the French President of the International Monetary Fund and the rape allegations with which he was charged. The ribbon at the bottom of the screen said 'Casey Stegall reports on IMF sex scandal.'

Sitting with me on the couch, Mom commented that it was a shame that men with money and power felt it was OK to behave this way.

"Between Arnold Schwarzenegger and Tiger Woods and Clinton and JFK, it's just criminal that they think they can get away with this stuff!"

"Yup," I agreed. "It's a real shame."

"And now it looks like Casey Stengel was involved in some kind of sex scandal."

"Who?" I asked, looking at the TV.

"You know, that guy, I think he was in baseball."

"You mean the Yankees manager, Casey Stengel?"

"Yes, him."

"Mom, I don't think Casey Stengel is still alive and if he was, he's probably be 90 or 100 years old! I think that's the name of the reporter."

"Well then he shouldn't be messing around at his age. And neither should that reporter!"

Life In An Elevator

GRUMPY GUY

The other morning as Bill came into the kitchen to refill his coffee, Mom commented "I guess that guy that shot that woman is crazy."

Confused, Bill asked "What guy? What woman?"

"You know, the astronaut's wife."

"Oh, you mean Loughner, the nut that shot Senator Giffords?"

"Yes, him. Plus he can't go to trial because he's in a bad mood."

"Bad mood?" Bill asked, even more confused.

"That's what they just said on the news," Mom answered. "He was in complaining."

"No they didn't," Bill replied. "They just said he was *incompetent* to stand trial."

"Well, maybe that's what put him in such a bad mood!"

Life In An Elevator

MERCURY RUN AMOK

While I was toasting a couple of English muffins for breakfast this past weekend, Mom commented on a story she'd just seen on TV.

"You know those crazy curly light bulbs we have to use," she started. "Well, they just said that when you use one you have to leave your house for 15 minutes because of the leaky mercury."

"You mean if you break one?" I asked. "I thought you had to clear out for a couple of hours and call in a haz-mat team to clean it up."

"No, they weren't talking about if it breaks, just when you turn the light on."

"Whoa, wait a minute. What do you mean 'turn it on?'"

"That's what they just said. Apparently, when you turn them on, they leak mercury. So you have to turn it off and leave your house for 15 minutes for the mercury fumes to clear."

"So every time you turn one of those stupid things on you have to immediately turn it off then leave your house?: I asked incredulously. "That's crazy."

"I guess so, since that's what they said. I think they need to get rid of the law. It's stupid. People shouldn't have to go outside every time they turn on a light."

"Yup, it sounds pretty inconvenient to me."

"And you just know," she continued, "people are going to throw them away and break them and there's going to be mercury loose everywhere."

"I think you're right, Mom. There's nothing worse than mercury run amok."

Life In An Elevator

THREE STOOGES

Sunday morning on Face the Nation, Bob Schieffer was interviewing several state governors, including Governor John Kasich of Ohio. Suddenly, Mom looked up from her scrambled eggs and started to snicker.

"What's so funny?" I asked.

"That he wants to put Obama in a nursing home," she said with a grin.

"What? Who?" I asked, almost choking on a bite of cantaloupe.

"Him," she said, waving her English muffin at Governor Kasich on the screen.

"No he didn't," I said. "He said Ohio's saving Medicaid money by letting mom and dad stay home instead of going into a nursing home."

"But his parents are dead, aren't they?" she asked.

"Who's parents?"

"Obama's."

"No, Mom. Anyone's parents."

"I thought his mother lived with him," piped in Bill.

"No, it's his mother-in-law," I said.

"Oh, the First Mother-in-Law," he replied.

"Who's first?" Mom asked.

"Michele's mother," Bill answered.

"Michele who?"

"You know, Mom, the First Lady."

"Oh. Is her mother in a nursing home too?"

I suggested that we change the channel. Maybe there was a Three Stooges rerun on somewhere. It would have made more sense.

Life In An Elevator

BOOBY TRAP

Out of nowhere last night, Mom asked "Did you know they have a new doll for little girls that comes with a bib that has a boob on it? I saw it on the news."

"The doll wears a bib that has a boob attached to it?" I asked.

"No, it's for the little girls to wear."

"What in the world for?" I exclaimed.

"So they can pretend to breast feed. The doll even burps!"

"Why would anyone want a little girl to practice breast feeding?"

"So they'll never, never, ever, ever forget how," she remarked, crossing her arms and bobbing her head for emphasis.

"Well, I think it's kind of creepy. Do you remember who the toy company is? I'll send them an email or write a letter."

"No, I don't. I just remember that it's some European company, which explains a lot," she huffed.

"I guess they're a lot more 'open-minded' about certain things," I said, trying to be politically correct.

"If by open-minded you mean stupid, then yes, they're more open-minded."

Life In An Elevator

SHERIFF JOE FOR PRESIDENT?

"There's a story coming up on the news about Sheriff Arpaio and his partner. Something about how they're not getting along," Mom announced when I brought her dinner in from the kitchen.

"His partner?" I asked. "Do you mean his ex-chief, Hendershott?"

"No, they said his partner," she insisted.

"His wife?" Bill asked.

"No, no, his partner. They said it very clearly. They're not getting along and have started drinking. Oh, look, here's the story."

We watched with rapt attention as the story unfolded. It was a piece about a new afternoon talk show on the local ABC affiliate, and the first person they interviewed was Sheriff Joe. They sound bite was from a discussion about, if Sheriff Joe was the president, how he would handle the problems with Congress' lack of *partisanship*. His solution was that everyone could get along if they just sat down over a *beer*.

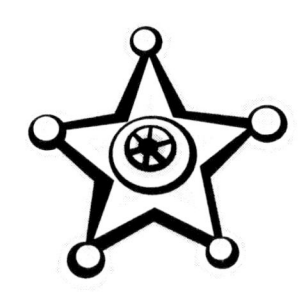

Life In An Elevator

MURDER'S AFOOT

I babysit our granddaughter twice a week, so instead of being tuned into a 24-hour news channel, 5-month old Olivia and I are glued to Sesame Street, Peppa Pig and Wow Wow Wubbzy. And during nap time, I gulp down a sandwich and try not to doze off. This is why your ovaries dry up and you can't have children after you reach a certain age. Watching an infant can wear you out. And I know that once she starts crawling and then walking, I'll either have to be in better shape or reconcile myself to spending the other three days a week in a recuperative coma.

My point is, I didn't know anything about Iranian assassins until I got home shortly before dinner time. Although watching the report on TV didn't seem to be necessary since Mom greeted me with the news flash as soon as I walked into the living room.

"Did you see the story about how they're trying to kill Iranians?" she asked as I walked into the house.

"No, Mom," I responded, collapsing into the recliner next to her couch.

"It was on the news at lunch time. They want to kill Iranians and they're using Mexicans to do it." She seemed almost giddy with excitement.

"Who's they," I asked.

"I don't know. I don't think they said. Just that our government found out about it."

"So I take it, our government stopped it."

"Maybe. I guess so. Although I don't know why they would. If Mexicans wanted to kill Iranians, I'd just let them."

At this point the five-o'clock news resumed from a commercial break on the living room television and they launched into a story about Homeland Security stopping a threat from Iranian assassins who were trying to murder the Saudi ambassador using killers from Mexican cartels.

Hi hon," Bill said, suddenly appearing from whatever part of the house he was hiding. He paused briefly to give me a peck on the cheek and a wink. "By the way, did you hear about the Mexicans that are trying to kill off the Iranians?" he called over his shoulder as he continued on his way to the kitchen.

"See," Mom called after me as I made my way to the liquor cabinet. "Bill heard it too!"

Life In An Elevator

On the Home Front

Life In An Elevator

MY MOM WON'T LET ME GET A PUPPY

Bill and I have always had a dog. Growing up, Bill had Heidi, his Dachshund. I had Dalmatians - Duchess and then Pepper. Mom even had a Cairn Terrier during her first years in Phoenix. My kids grew up with a Miniature Schnauzer followed by a Giant Schnauzer and they both have dogs now. Bill and I have had a Cocker and then two Bearded Collies - the absolute best, most amazing dogs ever. Our Beardies died shortly before we had to move to Arizona, which is probably a blessing since the summers here would have killed them any way.

After we'd been here a little over a year, I was getting the "itch." You animal lovers will relate. When a beloved pet dies, some people immediately get another because it fills an painful void and serves as a comfort. Others take longer, for whatever reasons - grief, misplaced guilt, fear of experiencing another lose. Whatever the cause, a true animal lover will ultimately crave the friendship, unconditional love and company of another pet. And that's what happened to me. I was done grieving and wanted a dog back in my life. And so did Bill. And like any good child, I asked my Mom if it was okay.

"Nope," she responded.

"Nope?" I repeated, somewhat stunned. "Why not. You love dogs."

"I do. You know I had a Fox Terrier growing up. And then I had Camie when I moved here."

"I remember her," I said. "She was a Toto dog. She was really smart but she liked to eat her own poop."

"Well, yes, that was one little problem. But she was great company before I remarried."

"So, why can't we get a dog?"

"Because I can't take care of a dog."

"No one's asking you to take care of it. That will be Bill's and my job. Just like we take care of everything else around here."

"But what if you go out, like to the store. I can't let it out if it has to pee."

"We're never gone that long. We'll let it out before we leave."

"What if you go away on a vacation someday?"

"We'll take it with us."

"What if you go spend the afternoon at the pool?"

Well, she sort of had us there. Now, I know what you're thinking. Cage train it. Get a doggy pee pad. Lock it in the garage. None of this logic mattered. She didn't want a dog. And to prove it, she started reading the Pet section of

33

Life In An Elevator

the want ads every Sunday and pointing out to us how expense dogs were. Purebreds cost a fortune; mutts were now Designer breeds and cost hundreds. Vets were expensive and what if something really terrible happened. We were on a fixed income. Her logic was infallible and decidedly daunting. But, damn it, I'm over 60 and I WANT A PUPPY. Maybe if I hold my breath until I turn blue?

Life In An Elevator

HAIRDRESSER MATH

On the way to the hairdresser, Mom commented on how pleased she was that her perm had lasted for four months.

"You know," she said. "I looked in my checkbook and I got this perm on February 7th."

"But Mom, this is May 6th, so it's only been three months, not four," I said.

"No, it's four," she countered. "February, March, April and May. Four."

"But this is only May 6th," I replied, holding up fingers. "February 7 to March 7 is one; March 7 to April 7 is two; April 7 to May 7 is three."

"But you have to count February as a month," she said. "So its four."

"No it isn't," I argued, counting on my fingers again. "February to March, March to April, April to May. Three months. It won't be four until June."

"But you have to count May as a month. February, March, April, May. Four months!"

My silence must have indicated agreement because the next response was a satisfied "Humf."

Life In An Elevator

THE SLIMFAST MYSTERY

Mom is a woman of rituals. Breakfast is a glass of OJ, a granola bar and a banana. Lunch is a can of chocolate Slimfast and a handful of flavored mini rice cakes. I love my mother, but this is a woman who needs Slimfast like Obama needs another birth certificate, but that's for another post. On an afternoon drive to her hairdresser, we had a conversation about the mystery of the disappearing diet drink.

"Now don't get mad, Patty," she began. "And don't say anything to Bill, but have you two been drinking my Slimfast?"

"No, why would you think that?"

"I noticed when I went into the refrigerator today for my Slimfast, that there was only one can left and the last time I counted there were five cans. Not that I mind, I was just wondering"

"Mom, look at me," I responded, indicating my avocado shaped, plus-size figure. "Do I look like I've been drinking Slimfast? "

" Maybe Bill's drinking it?"

"The only way Bill would touch that stuff is if it had tequila in it."

"Well it's not important, I just wanted to know where it's all going."

"Mom, I'm sure you just miscounted. When's the last time you took inventory."

"I thought it was this week. Maybe yesterday or the day before."

"Could it have been four or five days ago?"

"No, because then there'd be more cans gone."

"But Mom, I put five cans in on Sunday and this is Thursday."

"My point exactly!"

Life In An Elevator

LIFE IN AN ELEVATOR

When Bill and I moved here from Idaho, we transferred our satellite service. At first Mom refused to change from cable, so we had satellite on our TV in the Arizona Room and cable on hers in the Living Room. Eventually we won the argument that it was silly for her to pay for cable when we were paying for satellite. She relented and agreed to give it a try.

It took Mom awhile to adjust from the limitations of basic cable to the cornucopia of choices with satellite. At first she couldn't read the guide on the TV screen, so we replaced her old 36 inch mastodon with a 48 inch flat screen. Then she had trouble with the numbering scheme after years of cable memorization so we subscribed to the DirecTV Guide for her. And now, after a year and a half, she's almost got it figured out. She has the times and channel numbers of her favorite shows memorized and she's even discovered the wonderful world that the music channels have to offer.

She initially tried several genres - jazz, 60 and 70 oldies, big band, and show tunes. But she's finally settled on her favorite - Beautiful Instrumentals, aka elevator music. As a result, every afternoon the house fills with lilting, syrupy, and really loud elevator music. The volume is almost dance-club high. This is because, as Mom asserts, she's only a little deaf in her left ear and has decided she can hear just fine from her right ear so she doesn't need a hearing aid yet. She has, however, purchased several "over-the-counter" noise enhancers. The problem is, she never remembers to turn them off the battery operated units when she's done using them. And the two models that are rechargeable are constantly being plugged into the Kindle charger instead of the appropriate device's charger, so the batteries only last about a day and a half. At current count, she has three different types in the end table junk drawer next to her couch, two others mixed with the assorted clutter on the top of the table, and another on the nightstand next to her bed. And all six are deader than disco and there isn't a replacement battery in sight.

But back to the elevator music. The scary part is, Bill and I are starting to hum along with some of the tunes. Bill even found himself murmuring the lyrics to 'I Write The Songs' and, when he finally caught himself and realized - in horror - what he was doing, he immediately headed for the liquor cabinet. His rationale was that even though it was only 2:30 in the afternoon, if you count it as Sun City time, that's closer to 5:00 in the real world.

We both know our turn is around the bend, and in the future the house will be filled with loud 60's and 70's elevator music like "White Rabbit", "Light my Fire" and "Proud Mary" to the dismay of our kids who will be forced to listen to it.

37

Life In An Elevator

PUBLISHER'S CLEARINGHOUSE AND OTHER GAMES OF CHANCE

Mom is a proud Publisher's Clearinghouse groupie. She has been participating in their drawings for the last 50 years and wears this information like a badge of honor. The fact that she hasn't won ANYTHING seems to be irrelevant. When we first moved here, I had to clean out and consolidate her kitchen junk drawers. She had four - yes, count them - four junk drawers. And the reason was because of all the PCH stuff she orders.

For example, she had 12 packages of generic stain stick for your clothes. And each package contained a half dozen sticks. She had 4 boxes of super glue and each box held a dozen tubes. She had several envelope openers, 5 magnifying classes, each with a non-functional built-in light. There were 2 coin sorters and hundreds of empty paper coin rolls; 3 glasses repair kits; 4 travel-size tool kits plus 9 assorted screw drivers; there were instruction manuals for small appliances she no longer owned, wine bottle corks, spoon holders, 2 boxes of wooden matches, 3 staplers, a battery charger for an electric can opener that is nowhere to be found, and so much more.

And the junk drawer inventory was minor compared to the stash in the garage cabinets, the shelves in her bedroom closet and the drawer of her end table next to the couch. Let's just say that the eventual garage sale could probably have provided enough useless stuff to re-stock at least one PCH warehouse!

Each time she gets a "You Could Be The Next Big Winner!!" envelope, she has to remind me of her decades of loyalty.

"See, Patty," she says proudly. "I've been a member since 1961."

"Mom, I think 'member' is the wrong word," I counter, mumbling 'sucker' under my breath. "You haven't joined - you just continue to buy their stuff."

"I don't always buy something," she counters. "Sometimes I just send my entry back."

"Well, you buy enough so that you should have won something by now."

"But sometimes when I buy something, they send me a free gift."

"Like the free gift you got yesterday. What in the world are you going to do with an ice scraper? You don't have a car "

"But I got it for free and I gave it to Bill."

"Mom, we live in Phoenix! Besides, what did you have to buy to get that?"

"Toe Spreaders. They're suppose to separate my toes."

"And how's that working out?"

Life In An Elevator

"They seem to work fine until I take them off. Then my toes go back together."

"And for this you got a free ice scraper?"

"Yes, and a notice that I'm one of ten people in Arizona in the final drawing. Which reminds me, I need you to go to the post office for stamps. I'm almost out."

Life In An Elevator

THE PHONE BOOKS COMETH

We got another phonebook on the porch this morning. This is the fourth phonebook we've gotten in the last two weeks. It also follows a flurry of phonebook deliveries that came a few months ago. Apparently, the annual phone listing updates are now occurring bi-annually, and we're getting more books, more often - even though we haven't asked for them, ordered them or even want them. Mom suggested this would be a good time to weed out the old phone books until Bill reminded her that the ones we have are only two-weeks old since we weeded out then.

"At least we don't get a lot of door-to-door salesmen here" she continued. " That's one of the benefits of living in Sun City. They just seem to stay away."

"Oh," replied Bill. "I guess you're not including all the roofing companies that have descended on us like locust since February."

"Well," she answered, "besides them we don't get anyone else."

"What about all the landscapers" I asked.

"Oh, they just want to trim the trees. Besides them, we don't get anyone else."

"What about the handymen. I bet Bill and I have turned away a dozen just this year."

"They just want to paint the house. That's how I did it before. Someone came to the door and offered to paint."

"OK," I said, "but our house is newly painted. And we have new windows. And we haven't got trees to trim since we put in the desert landscaping."

"At least we don't get a lot of the religious people coming to the door," she said. "That's a good thing."

"That because you never answer the door, Mom" Bill responded. "I've turned away Mormons, Baptists and last week there was a van full of Jehovah's Witnesses that swarmed the neighborhood. But other than that, I guess we don't get any religious people coming to the door."

"That's right," she answered, somewhat smugly. "Just like I said, we don't have to worry about being bothered by people coming to the door because we live in Sun City."

Life In An Elevator

LAST WOMAN STANDING

When Bill and I moved in with Mom, we converted the third bedroom into a home office. When we are in between contracts (which is the majority of the time lately), we spend most mornings in here goofing off on our computers. We read Drudge, check out Groupon, read email, see what's happening on Facebook, and generally feign busy-ness in order to drown out Mom's TV noise, which is always turned on and always *LOUD*. So, in order to *not* hear the Price Is Right screaming that accompanies "come on down" and the audience shouting each contestants response on Family Feud (name a type of job: oil - OIL, nose - NOSE, boob - BOOB).

Mom usually wanders in a couple of time each morning to give us important updates like "I'm getting dressed now," or "I'm taking a shower now," or "do you have a job now?" This morning she got a phone call from an old friend in Michigan, so she wandered back to the office to fill us in.

"That was Lil," she announced. "And the news is we're about the only ones left!"

"Well that's too bad," I said. "But Lil's okay?"

"Yes. And so is Priscilla. Except she's has peripheral vision."

"You mean she's losing her peripheral vision?" I asked.

"No, she's going blind in her peripheral parts."

"Does she have cataracts?"

"No, she has blindness. It's just her peripherals right now."

"Her peripherals are going blind?"

"No, her eyes. Her peripherals are OK. Plus no one knows what happened to Dorothy."

"Dorothy Fairbanks?"

"Yes. She died but it's a mystery. No one knows how. And Elaine Rouseau fell down in the bathtub."

"Didn't she get pneumonia?"

"No, she died in the tub and just fell down. So there just aren't that many of us left. Oh by the way, I'm taking a shower now."

41

Life In An Elevator

THE MAGICAL FRUIT

I don't understand bananas. Bill and I were grocery shopping and we had to replenish Mom's banana supply. We used to go to the grocery store several times a week just to make a banana run for Mom until finally, after much experimentation and trial and error, we came up with a semi-scientific method of banana management.

First, we have to factor in how many bananas are currently ripening on the kitchen counter. Then we have to determine their 'brownage' factor. If we conclude that they're verging on being too brown for Mom to consider eatable, we have to eliminate them from the on-hand inventory count because there is a point of brownage from which there is no return and they get thrown in the trash. Then we have to weigh the greenishness of the bananas on display in the produce department and evaluate the length of time remaining until they reach the over-brownage factor. We try to buy just enough to get up to, but not beyond, optimum brownage. And finally, we have to select the perfect size. Large bananas are out because Mom can't eat more than about 6 inches of fruit. We've tried getting bigger, but really curvy bananas so they don't look longer, but she's on to us and complains every morning while she's peeling.

"Honey," she laments. "These are just too big and I can't eat it all. I hate to waste it, but I know I'm going to throw part of it away."

I'm not sure why, along with her little breakfast bar and glass of orange juice, she can't eat another 2 inches of banana. It's truly a digestive mystery since at dinner she can snarf down a half slab of ribs, coleslaw, and camp potatoes and still have room for two scoops of mint-chocolate chip ice cream!

But, back to the produce department. Besides the Ensure shelves, the banana display is the most popular place in the Sun City Safeway. Seniors gather here in droves. It's like a RAVE for the geriatric set. They talk about the latest cruise they were on, brag about grand children, discuss politics and candidates, and complain about the lack of handicapped parking spots.

They hover over the green and yellow bunches, using their own system of fruit selection. The banana display is always piled high with fruit - unless it's on sale. Then, within minutes after the produce manager has stocked the bins, they're instantly emptied by grasping, shoving seniors. A mark down of 59 a pound to 49 a pound is tantamount to a banana tsunami. And if it's Senior Discount Day on top of a sale - well you might as well stay home because I think they actually lay in wait by the back loading bay and attack the Chiquita delivery truck before it can even be unloaded.

Anyway, as I said at the beginning of this rather rambling conversation, Bill and I don't understand bananas. They're like crack for seniors. They *must* have their bananas every single day. They don't go crazy for apples or grapes or oranges. Grapefruit, cantaloupe, peaches and pears seem to have

Life In An Elevator

only a mild appeal. They will, however, attack you over a strawberry sale (see The Great Strawberry War for the gory details). So what is it that keeps them coming back for the bananas? Potassium? Memories of past loves? Symbolically stripping the wrapping off a pale, creamy body? We just don't know. Maybe the Bobbers could tell us, but, quite frankly, we're afraid to ask. I hope if Bill and I ever start to yearn for a daily banana it's well blended inside a Daiquiri.

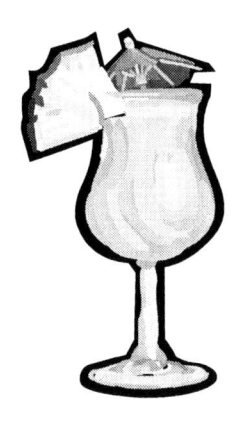

Life In An Elevator

MEAN, GREEN ICE CREAM MACHINE

When the grand kids visit, Bill and I make them help by doing little things. They have to take their plates into the kitchen when they're done eating dinner. Why, you might ask, aren't they eating in the kitchen in the first place? Because, I would remind you, Mom insists on eating dinner in front of the TV in order to watch the 6:00 news and Wheel of Fortune. Our 9-year old grand-daughter, Amber, loves Wheel of Fortune, so this is a plus. Jack, our 6 year-old grandson thinks it's stupid and Pat Sajak is 'creepy' so he usually snarfs down his dinner so he can escape into the office and play on Papa's PC. But I'm rambling.

Other little chores we have them do is take Mom's dinner plate to her, bring it back to the kitchen when she done eating, and deliver the required nightly bowl of Mint Chocolate Chip ice cream to her. And why, you may ask, is this a requirement? Because, for as long as we've lived here, this is what Mom has *every single night* after dinner. Even if we go out to eat, when we get home, she has to have her bowl of Mint Chocolate Chip ice cream. One time, we bought a brand that didn't dye the ice cream green. It was a name-brand and quite good when I tasted a blob that had fallen off the ice cream scoop onto the counter. But, until the half gallon was depleted of its treat, she continued to insist each night, either when I brought her the full bowl or took the empty away, that it was vanilla ice cream because it was white! Anyway, I'm rambling again.

During the kids last visit, it was Jack's turn to take Granny her ice cream. As he handed it to her he commented, "Granny, that's my favorite kind. Except for the triple chocolate blizzard at Dairy Queen, which is awesome." And then he left to wash up since we were taking them to Dairy Queen for awesome blizzards.

Like most 6-year-old boys, Jack's hand washing consists of a pass-through under the faucet, a quick handshake, and a high-five pat on the towel. All-in-all, a 23 second ritual. Amber on the other hand, washes daintily, dries thoroughly, brushes her hair, tries on a couple of hair scrunchies, picks out a pair of colorful wrist bangles and changes her clothes because what she had on didn't match the bangles. This take about 20 minutes.

While we were waiting for Amber, Jack passed back through the living room on his way to the PS3 in the family room when he passed by Granny, who apparently was scraping the last remaining chocolate bits from her now empty bowl.

"Boy, Granny," Jack said. "You must really like that ice cream because you ate it all really fast. My mom yells at me when I eat too fast. She says my tummy won't know I'm full and it'll make me fat. I guess that's what happened to you." And then he smiled sweetly as he took the bowl and headed to the kitchen.

Life In An Elevator

She looked at me quizzically and mouthed 'fat?' to which I shook my head.

"Mom," I said, trying to think of a appeasing response. "You just look spread out when you're sitting. It's the curse of the Carpenter hip."

"Well, at least I'm not like those women on the Price Is Right." she retorted. "Now they're fat!"

Life In An Elevator

HELP I'VE FALLEN AND I CAN'T STOP TALKING ABOUT IT

Mom has a tendency to fall down. Before she got her walker, it was a lot. Maybe half a dozen times a month. Now that she's decided to make her walker her best friend, it only happens once every four to six weeks. Fortunately, Mom is blessed because the women in our family have strong bones. Plus, Mom is pretty well padded around her middle, her hips and her butt - so when she goes down, she lands more like a beach ball than an anvil.

She does bruise quite easily though. This is because, like many elderly folks, her skin is gradually turning to rice paper and her veins are closer to the surface that they were in her youth. She can bump the back of her hand against the armrest on her loveseat and she'll raise an attractive purple contusion. She can nudge her leg against the bed mattress and get a lovely black and blue shiner on her knee. So, when she falls down, absolutely remarkable welts and bruises form on the parts of her body that made contact with any object that's harder than a cotton ball. She wears the temporary discoloration like badges of honor and shows them off with pride. And she isn't particularly shy about showing me where each and every bruise is, if you get my drift.

She took a tumble a week ago getting up from her nap. She sat up too quickly and then tried to stand. This resulted in a brief dizzy spell that caused her to plop back onto the couch, then roll off the edge, fall onto the carpeting and whack her leg on the marble base of the coffee table.

A few days after this latest tumble, I was in the living room, gathering her morning paper to put in the recycle bin, when she stopped me before I could escape to the safety of the garage.

"Patty, look at this bruise," she said, pulling up her blouse so I could see the Italy-shaped greenish-yellow blob along her rib cage.

"That's a good one, Mom," I comment, turning to leave.

"And this is where my leg hit the table," she bragged, lifting her pant leg so I could see the marks on her shin.

"It's pretty well faded, isn't it?" I ask, backing slowly away, praying silently that this was the end of the damage.

"And I think this is where I landed on the floor," she continued, pulling her blouse above her bra. Before she could shift the bra out of the way, I back peddled, muttering "Looks good, Mom. You're sure lucky to be so bouncy."

"I know," she said, smiling broadly. "It runs in the family, so when you start falling down you should be okay too."

Life In An Elevator

"Good to know," I said, walking quickly out of the room. "...I'll keep that in mind the next time I decide to try bungee jumping," I muttered.

Life In An Elevator

SUN CITY LOCK DOWN

Living in Sun City means living behind securely locked, iron-barred security doors and dead bolts that are firmly latched and windows that are <u>never</u> opened to allow a fresh, cool fall breeze to flow through the house - unless you have burglar bars installed. However, leaving the garage door up a foot or so to help keep air - or critters - circulating inside is permitted. And so is having a sun porch that is encased in window screen that can be pushed out of the aluminum frame by an angry finch.

Mom's latest bug-a-boo is the lock on the sliding glass door that opens into our sun porch. She's suddenly decided it needs to be locked all the time, even when Bill and I are home and sitting in the room. It doesn't matter that we're working outside and are coming and going through the sun porch, into the Arizona room and then into the garage. It doesn't matter that it's broad daylight, the sheriff who lives four houses away has his car parked in his driveway, and neighbors are walking their dogs and chatting on the sidewalk. The garage door must be down, ALL the locks on ALL the doors and windows must be in place, double-checked, and remain that way - ALL THE TIME. It makes going outside for more than 3 minutes difficult and makes coming back in even harder since she tends to wander around after we've gone outside and lock the doors, completely forgetting that we're still home, just not in the house. This leads to ringing the front doorbell, waiting for her to retrieve her walker and make her way to the foyer, waiting while she looks out the peephole, then waiting some more while she unlocks the two locks on the front door, followed by the security door deadbolt and the lock on the door handle.

And she never fails to look surprised to see us. For example, a couple of evenings ago we were talking to our neighbor, Art. When we tried going back inside, we discovered she'd locked the patio door. We trudged around the house and found the garage door was down and the front door was locked. So Bill rang the doorbell.

"What are you doing out here?" she asked, once she finally managed to get both doors opened.

"We were in back talking to Art and you locked us out," Bill said, wiping sweat out of his eyes. "Why do you have to have everything locked up tight when we're home?" he asked, somewhat testily.

"Because, you never know who's going to break in and steal your stuff. That happens to old people all the time here, I know because I read the crime statistics in the paper" she replied.

"If you're nervous we can get an alarm," offered Bill, even though she turned it down when we suggested bringing our alarm system from our house in Boise.

Life In An Elevator

"No, I don't want one of those things. They're loud and they don't always work and they cost money. Besides, I've got you and Bill," she continued. Little does she know that Bill, the coward that he is, is more likely to shout out "Shoot her first, she's old" while diving through the broken - but still locked - window that the intruder came through.

"Bill and I being here doesn't help if you keep us locked outside," I argued. "You know, the best deterrent to a burglar is a dog. We could get a dog," I said hopefully, trying again for the puppy she won't let me have.

"No, I told you before, I can't take care of a dog," she announced, then turned abruptly and shouted out "LAS VEGAS STRIP TEASE!" smiling proudly as she solved the latest Wheel of Fortune puzzle.

Life In An Elevator

I HEAR VOICES

At least twice a week, Mom wakes up to a new noise. And every time it happens, she asks Bill if he heard it. I guess this is because he's up at 5:30 and I usually sleep in until 6:30 or 7:00. This morning she came out of her bedroom at 7:15 and walked across the hall into our office where we were checking email

"Did you hear a loud horn around 6:00?" she asked Bill.

"Nope," he replied, double-clicking on another piece of spam.

"'It was like a car horn but really long," she added.

"It might have been a car alarm,: I offered. "Maybe the people who talk outside your bedroom window bumped a car on their way towards the house."

"Oh, I doubt that," she said. "They're usually there around 5 or so. Besides, I didn't hear anyone talking today, just the horn."

"Maybe it was so loud you couldn't hear them talking?" I said, joking with her a bit.

"Maybe," she replied seriously, actually thinking about it. "Why, did you hear them talking this time, Bill?"

"Nope," he grunted, closing Mail and opening Explorer.

"I just don't understand how you never hear anything outside. Especially the screaming. I'm surprised the police didn't come when I heard that last week."

"Screaming?" I asked, glancing over my shoulder at Bill. He just shrugged and logged onto his Amazon account.

"Yes, screaming," she said, nodding her head for emphasis. "I got up to pee around 2:00 in the morning like I usually do and someone was screaming right outside the bathroom window. I can't believe neither one of you heard it."

"Well then, you must hear the garbage trucks every Tuesday and Friday at 6:30," Bill interjected.

"No, I roll over on my good ear, so I never hear them." And with that she toddled out of the room, heading toward the kitchen and her crossword.

"Bill," I whispered, swiveling my chair around to face him. "She's hearing stuff a lot lately. What do you think it is?"

"I haven't got a clue," he muttered, opening my blog window to check my readership stats. "Maybe the new clock radio we got her plays weird sounds."

Life In An Elevator

I actually gave that a few seconds of serious thought, debated whether or not to check it out, then realized he was kidding.

"Interesting idea," I said. "Instead of ocean waves and rain it plays car alarms and screaming. I think you're on to something. Quick, email Brookstone!"

Life In An Elevator

MARTHA STEWART HAS LEFT THE BUILDING

My Mom has nothing on Martha Stewart. Before we moved here, she'd was able to artlessly blend the harvest gold's and avocado green's of the seventies with the mauves, slate blues and grays of the eighties and achieve a design balance that captured the absolute worst of both decades. And she even managed to include op art from the psychedelic sixties. Her blend of Danish Modern, Oriental, and Adams Family-inspired decor - all in one room - created an ambience that was both amazingly unattractive and bewildering in its lack of style and good taste. Someone who hasn't seen it might wonder if this was intentionally eclectic. Sadly, it isn't. It's just ugly.

And then there is her love affair with sponge painting, a nineties phenomena. When she moved into the house in '92 she sponged the walls of the guest bath - which is now our bathroom - in sea green and bright, cotton candy pink, and adorned the walls with ceramic angles, cherubs and embroidered fish. And she didn't stop there. She also painted the bathroom door, the trim and molding, the ceiling, the cabinet (inside and out), the ceiling vent fan and every hinge in the room, pink. She completed her decorating tour-de-force by covering the floor with a cheap wall-to-wall rug remnant of fuzzy, avocado green, rubber-backed nastiness. And to further add to the general appeal, the bathroom was equipped with a 40-year old tub-shower combo that had textured plastic sliding doors that had been re-caulked so often, and so poorly, that there was a thick, irregular ribbon of grayish goo along every seam.

A few months after we'd moved in with Mom, Bill and I came home with paint chips and cabinet brochures and dreams of remodeling the hideousness we had to face daily. We were comparing colors against the existing, yellowing faux-marble counter top and the asbestos-based gray and yellow linoleum that had been successfully hiding for two decades under the puke-green rug, when Mom wandered down the hall and squeezed her way into the room.

"What are you two up to?" she said.

"Looking at paint colors," I answered.

"What are you going to paint," she asked, sudden suspicion in her voice.

"The bathroom," Bill responded, placing a chip on the far wall near the floor.

"And why exactly would you do that?" she said defensively.

"Oh I don't know," I said, totally oblivious to the can of worms Bill and I had opened. "Maybe because everything in here is pink. And I'm not too crazy about pink. Or sponge painting for that matter."

" Well I like pink," she stated firmly. "And I think this room looks just fine and sponging is one of the latest ways to paint and besides that, I did it all by myself!"

Life In An Elevator

"Latest way maybe twenty years ago," Bill muttered before I had a chance to kick him in the shin.

"Okay, Mom," I said, trying to calm her down. "I didn't know you liked it so much. We'll live with it for a while longer."

"That would be nice, but you do what you want. It's your bathroom after all."

We lived with it another year until the fiberglass base in the tub 'accidently' cracked badly enough that we had to put in a nice, new shower unit - which somehow didn't match anything else in the room. Oh, my, what a shame.

Life In An Elevator

PATTY'S TATTIE

Bill and I were getting ready to go to the pool and I was wandering through the house in my bathing suit, filling our go-cups with Crystal Lite and bagging up some Cheeze Doodles for munching. I had made my way through the living room and was heading for the kitchen, when a sudden shriek stopped me in my tracks.

"Patty Ann! What on earth is that on your back?"

Fearing a black widow or scorpion had landed on me, I started turning around like a dog chasing its tail, frantically brushing at my shoulders.

"Where? Where?" I yelled. "What is it? A bug?"

"No," she answered. "It's a picture of something."

I stopped twirling and breathed a sigh of relief. "Do you mean my tattoo?" It's on my right shoulder blade and is about 2 inches around.

"Yes. When in the world did you get that? Have you lost your mind?"

"Mom," I answered. "I've had it for years."

"No you haven't," she argued. "I'd have noticed it before."

"You have," I replied. "Every time you walk in on me when I'm getting dressed you ask about it. And every time I tell you the same thing. I got it one time when we were at our timeshare in the Cayman's. I was 56 and having a post-mid-life-getting-older-and-fatter crisis. It's the same year I learned how to dive."

"And you're lucky you didn't get eaten by a shark!"

"I know, Mom, they're lurking everywhere just waiting to eat over weight, middle-aged, novice SCUBA divers," I said sarcastically.

"Well, I think tattoos are ridiculous," she snorted. "What's it supposed to be?"

"It's a Butterfly Fish and Bill designed it and I like it."

"And what's it going to look like when you're old and wrinkled?"

"I don't know, Mom. Maybe it'll turn into a Flounder!"

Life In An Elevator

TIME OUTS FOR EVERYONE!

There are days when I'm convinced I'm living with two children, namely my mom and my husband. For some reason Mom has become somewhat OCD about making sure all the doors and windows are locked up tight night and day. Bill and I always make sure that, whenever we leave the house to run errands, everything is locked so that when we say "we're running errands" and she inevitably asks, "is everything locked up" we can honestly answer yes. Then, once were gone, she totters around checking all the locks anyway. We know this because we've staked out the house and watched her, partly because we want to make sure she doesn't fall down and partly because it's starting to drive Bill nuts. And what's really fueling his lunacy is that she does it even when we're home.

For example, every night when she comes into the Arizona Room to say good night to us, she always, *always* asks if the patio door is locked. And I always, *always* tell her the same thing, which is yes. Then she totters over to the door and jiggles the lock to make sure I'm not lying. It's really making Bill crazy.

I know I talked about this phenomenon in Sun City Lock Down, but this goes beyond the typical cautions that the elderly take and is verging on paranoia. And did I mention that it's *driving Bill crazy.*

So now, to help retain his sanity, Bill is reverting to childish behavior and that has resulted in the two-child household I now find myself living in. For example, it can be the middle of the morning and Bill and I are watching something riveting on TV, like Sponge Bob, and Mom will wander into the Arizona Room and lock the patio door. As soon as she leaves, Bill jumps up and unlocks it. Then, when Mom goes into the kitchen at lunch time for her Slim Fast and rice cakes, she make a side trip into the Arizona Room and locks the door. This will prompt Bill to stop whatever it is he's doing, no matter where he is in the house, and tip-toe into the Arizona Room and unlock the door. Then there's Mom's pre-nap lock check, followed quickly by Bill's unlocking ritual, Mom's post-nap lockup, Bill's unlocking, Mom pre-dinner... well, you get the picture. And once the weather starts to cool in October and November to the 70's during the day and the 50's at night, it will get even crazier because Bill likes to leave the windows opened to let in the wonderful Arizona winter breezes. And, since it's more difficult for Mom to slide the windows closed through the wooden blinds, she'll constantly be calling for me to shut the windows.

I've tried to reassure Mom. I've tried to reason with Bill. I've yelled at both of them and even attempted to give them each time outs. And, no, that didn't work out real well. At this point, I'm ignoring them both. I figure all this up and down and traipsing in and out of the Arizona Room is the only exercise either one of them gets.

55

Life In An Elevator

The Bobbers

Life In An Elevator

THE BOBBERS

Bill and I have joined a gang. We don't wear colors and we don't have to get matching tats, but we all hang out together in the big pool during the sweltering hot Arizona summer days. The gang is called the Bobbers because it's what we do... bob around in the water talking Sun City trash.

The main-stays of the group are Paul, Jim, Ron, Barb, Evelyn, Marge and the dominatrix Sylva. Sylva is a very tall, stately lady of Baltic origin and unknown age. She body is tanned nut-brown and her brown hair is streaked with golden salon highlights. She wears her two piece bathing suits with pride. She doesn't seem to care that gravity has won in the battle with her ample bosoms, which are resting peacefully on the shelf made by her not-so-taut tummy. She keeps the Bobbers in line in between smoke breaks in the 5 x 5 smoking area in the back corner of the pool complex while staying hydrated drinking a pale green concoction that she pours frequently and liberally into a plastic cup.

Yesterday as we bobbed around in a loosely formed circle, the subject of bunnies came up. As I've mentioned before, rabbits are a terrible problem here. Bill was under the impression that the Sun City rabbits were focusing on our yard, to the exclusion of the rest of the homes here. Ron was talking about building a six-foot block fence around his lot, but his neighbors weren't too happy about that. I asked why a three foot fence wouldn't work.

"Oh no, honey," said Evelyn. "The bunnies jump right over that. I know because our neighbor has one and it doesn't help a bit."

"I used to feed them," Barb interjected.

"You mean like leftover salad stuff?" I asked. "I used to do that when I thought they were cute."

"Oh no, dear," she said. "We started out with that, but then we'd buy rabbit food at Pet Smart . But that wasn't enough, because they started eating my petunia and the marigolds. And they aren't even suppose to like marigolds. That's when I said enough is enough."

"So, how'd you get them to stop?" I asked, hoping the secret would finally be revealed.

"We built a six foot wall around our property."

"Well, I guess that would do it," I replied.

"Not quite. We had to put chicken wire on all the drainage holes around the base of the wall because they came in there."

"So, that fixed it?"

"Sort of. What we didn't know was we walled one of them in and it took us a couple of months to figure it out. Then we had to leave the gate open and

Life In An Elevator

herd the little sucker out, which took about four hours and almost gave my husband a stroke. But now, finally, we're in a bunny free zone!"

Later, as Bill and I were leaving, he looked at me with sad eyes and said "so, it isn't only us, is it."

"No honey, that's what I've been trying to tell you. The bunnies aren't just picking on you. They're out to get everyone."

"Does this mean I can't get a BB gun?"

"Bill, we've talked about this. You'll shoot your eye out!"

Life In An Elevator

THE MAD HATTER

Bill has a favorite cap. It's the one he got for free from the American Home Brewer's Association at least a decade ago when he was actively - and vigorously - making his own beer. The beer was excellent; he made a Saison to die for and his Wheat could have won awards. But he had to stop when gout, which is triggered by beer, became a problem. Fortunately, rum and Coke don't seem to cause this problem.

Anyway, Bill always wear this hat to the pool. He straps it to the back of his chair while we're in the water and usually puts it on once we're back in our lounge chairs. Yesterday he forgot and left the hat hooked onto the back of the chair when we left. We weren't too concerned, however; after all, this is Sun City and we just knew some nice retiree would turn it into lost and found and we could pick it up the next time we went to the rec center - which turned out to be the next day.

We explained what had happened the day before to the receptionist and she directed us to the lost and found. It turned out to be a cardboard box in the corner of the workout room. There were several towels, a couple pairs of sun glasses, a set of sponge hair rollers and an empty plastic container that was shaped to hold a set of dentures. How do I know this? Because the faded print on the top of the flesh-colored box said 'Chopper Hopper.'

Our faith in senior citizenship fading, we made our way to the far end of the pool where the lounge chairs we'd used were sitting unoccupied. Before we could get all the way to the row of chairs, Sylva (*see "The Bobbers" blog*) came rushing out from her smoking corner, waving at us.

"Ha Lo, ha lo," she called to us. "I knew you vud be back. Look vat I haf for you." she sang, reaching into her enormous beach tote and bringing out Bill's hat, which she proceeded to wave over her head.

"Some old fart vas trying taking it, but I stopped him! He vas going to vear it right outta here," she continued. "But I stepped into his face and said 'STOP! Dat is not yours. Give it to me.' And I took it from him, like DAT," she said whipping it in front of Bill's face and snapping the fingers of her free hand.

"Sylva, thank you so much," Bill said, smiling broadly. He tried to reach out for the hat, but Sylva is a good head taller than both Bill and me, so we knew that, until she'd finished her story and lowered her arm, the hat was out of reach.

"He vas no regular, he vas a stinkin' Snow Bird, I bet. When I yelled STOP he got red and ven I said 'dat hat is NOT yours, gimme it' and he handed it over quick an den he skunked away."

"Thanks, so much," Bill said, reach tentatively for the hat.

"Vat else is dare to do! You're a Bobber. You're vone of us. Vee take care of each otter. Right?"

Life In An Elevator

"Right, Sylva," Bill replied, stretching his reach toward the cap. "And thanks again, so much."

"You betcha sveetie," she said, finally handing it to Bill. As he reach to take it from her, she grabbed him by the wrist and pulled him in for a hug, giving me a wink over the top of his head. I smiled back at her and hoped she'd release Bill soon - I don't think he was getting much air buried between Sylva's ample boobs.

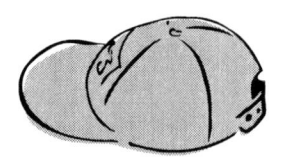

Life In An Elevator

SUN CITY TRIVIA

Remember the TV shows you loved when you were young? Then you better write them down or be prepared for a rousing game of 'Sun City Trivia' someday when you least expect it. Bobbing with the bobbers one Saturday in July, a sudden outbreak of nostalgia rippled through the water like a pebble splash in a pond.

"Remember Uncle Miltie?" Marge asked no one in particular.

"Oh yeah, the umm, the Texaco something," responded Rodger.

"Texaco Star Hour," said Bill.

"Right, that's the ticket. And how about Red Skelton. His show was really great."

"And so was Gleason. What was that one?" the other Bill interjected.

"The Honeymooners," answered Bill.

"That's it. I loved that show," chimed in Rodger's wife Irene. "And I really like that one with Donald Howard."

"Who," I asked.

"You know, he was a little kid and his father was the sheriff. Was it Bob Newton?"

"You mean Bob Newhart? No, it was Ron Howard and Andy Griffith. Andy of Mayberry," said Bill.

"That's who I meant," Irene said. "And that Bob Newton's show was really good too."

"*Newhart*," I offered, winking at Bill. " So was Carol Burnett."

"Tim Connelly and Harry Korman were the best," added Irene

"Boy I'll say," said Paul. "Those two just cracked me up."

Bill rolled his eye at me and muttered "Tim *Conway* and *Harvey* Korman."

"Aren't they dead?" asked Marge. "I think just about everyone's dead."

"Tim Conway's still alive. And so is Carol Burnett." I said. "She was on an episode of Glee last season."

"Glee?" the other Bill, Paul and Marge asked at once.

"Yeah, it's a show about a Glee Club. It's really funny and the music is great. It's very popular."

"When's it on?" asked Rodger.

"Wednesdays at 7:00," Bill said.

Life In An Elevator

"Oh well, we watch Lawrence Welk on PBS then."

"I know, isn't he wonderful?" said Marge, almost swooning. "I think it's amazing he's still on the air. I guess he's just, you know, just... ummm, what's that word?"

"Dead?" I asked.

"No, no, that other word that means, you know, that something's been around a lot."

"Promiscuous?" Bill whispered. He then offered aloud "timeless?"

"That's it," shouted Marge. "Timeless. He's, um... oh crap, who were we talking about?"

Life In An Elevator

TUMMY TUCKS ARE FOR SISSIES

Bill and I were at our favorite rec center on Sunday, lounging in the cool water, chatting and laughing with a gaggle of bobbers. And holding court, as always, was Sylva, the matriarch of the Bell Recreation Center. Everyone knows Sylva. It isn't because she's almost six feet tall. It isn't because she weighs in at around 190 soaking wet (which she usually is). It isn't because she's tanned mahogany-brown and pours her size 18 body into size 14 two-piece swimsuits. No, it isn't for any of these reasons. It's because Sylva says so - loudly, proudly and often.

When not in the water, she holds court in the southwest corner, under the cement awning in the only smoking spot in the entire center, chain smoking and sipping whatever adult beverage she's brought that day in her thermos.. From here she has an unobstructed view of the large pool, the walking pool to the northeast, all of the dozens and dozens of lounge chairs scattered throughout the cool decking and, most importantly, the entrance from the clubhouse. She's admitted to Bill and me that she is addicted to the pool.

"Sveetie, I come here every day no matter vhat."

"Even in the winter?" Bill asked.

"Yes, most certainly. Even in da cold, da rain and even in da dust storms. Dey make me go ven it's da thunda and lightening. I try to say no, no Sylva vill stay, but dey make me leaf. Fockin' cowards is vat dey are!"

That's Sylva's favorite word - f***. She uses it as a noun, a verb, an adverb and a pronoun. For example, Bill and I were winding our way back to our lounge chairs after getting out of the pool when she called me over.

"Sveetie, come here."

I'm sveetie, Bill's darlink, that's how I knew she wanted me. I gave Bill a pleading look, but he just stifled a laugh and kept on walking.

"What's up, Sylva?" I asked, as I entered the smoking zone.

Putting a motherly arm around my shoulders, she asked "Vat size svimsuit do you vear?"

"I don't know, I try not to think about it. I guess a large - maybe extra large."

"Vell, I haf a suit I vant you to try on. It's not black like you wear. It has focking colors like I wear. You know, like tiger and leopard. Dis one for you is like snake. You vill like it because it vill hold you in."

"Hold me in where?" I asked, knowing there were many parts of my body that could benefit from being 'held in.'

"Here, sveetie," she said, patting me soundly on the tummy. "Such a nice face, you should suck dat focker in and dis suit vill help. Also, da undervear at Valmart verks too."

Life In An Elevator

"Underwear?" I whispered.

"Ya. You get dat kind vat goes from your boobs to your butt. Dat vill keep dat focker sucked in."

"Okay. For under clothes, right?"

"Nah, for under focking everyting, even swim suits. And get some for darlink. He's too good lookin' for such a focking big stomach."

So there I was, walking back toward Bill and our lounge chairs, after having someone I've known for just a couple of weeks tell me that my husband and I are fat. How depressing is this?

I told the story to Bill, who immediately got defensive

"We don't look any different than anyone else at the pool and besides I've worked very hard for the last 24 years of our marriage to get my stomach into this perfectly round condition," he said defensively. "And I'm pretty damn proud of it and I'm proud of you and I think you look perfect the way you are."

"Do we have any more Cheeze Doodles in the beach bag?" I asked, giving him a well-deserved hug. At least my honey loves me the way I am.

Life In An Elevator

MEMORIES - GOING, GOING, GONE

Bill and I were at the pool this past weekend, bobbing around with some of the Bobbers. There was Roger and his wife Irene, Marge, Rose, another Bill, and Paul. We were commenting on the limited summer fare on TV.

"I watched that show you recommended," Marge said to me. "You know, Eckles."

"Echoes?" I asked.

"No, Eckles or Eeckles. You know, the one with the two women."

"Oh, you mean Rizzoli and Isles."

"Yes. Eckles, Isles, close enough. Anyway, it was pretty good."

"Don't forget The Glades tonight," I reminded her. "It's pretty good too."

"Remember when there were really good programs on TV," said Roger. "Like the original Hawaii Five-0. The new one sucks."

"Well, James Caan's son is good," I commented. "What's his name? Sean? Todd?" I asked, looking at Bill for help.

"Scott."

"Right, Scott. And there's always Blue Bloods. I mean really, anything with Tom Sellack is good."

Every female head nodded enthusiastically. "What about his old program?" asked Irene. "You know, the one in Hawaii."

"Magnum PI," said Bill.

"Right. And what was that other one, honey?" I asked. "You know, the detective one where he had the black secretary."

"Maddox." he said.

"That's it. And what about that other one. You know the one they filmed in Vegas at that really nice, modern-looking hotel."

"What hotel?" asked the other Bill.

"I'm not sure. Wait, wait, ummm, it was glass and sometimes if you got to town at the right time, you'd catch them filming. And his car was always parked out front. Did I say it was glass? Desert something maybe," I said.

"Dunes?" asked Roger

"Nope. Gone," said Marge.

"Sahara?"

"Gone."

65

Life In An Elevator

"Sands?"

"Gone."

"Flamingo?"

"Gone."

"Wait, wait," I interrupted. "It was the Desert Inn."

"Gone," chimed in Irene and the other Bill.

"Ok, but the show was filmed there back in the late 70's or early 80's. I can see the guy's face. His son's an actor and he's got a funny name."

"Funny?" asked Bill. "Funny like what?"

"I don't know, just funny - different. It's Skippy or Scooter or something like that."

"Okay," Bill said. "Different like Skippy and his father's an actor too."

"Yes, but I think he's dead."

"Who, Scooter?" asked Irene.

"No, his father," I said.

"Alright, let me get this straight," Bill interjected. "It's a show that used to be on with a dead actor who's son is named Skippy. Have I got it all?"

"No, he was a detective and he drove a really cool care and it also used to be filmed at the Desert Inn, but that's been blown up."

"So Skipper/Scooter's dead dad filmed a detective TV series in Vegas driving a really cool car at a blown-up hotel"

"Skeech!" I yelled.

"God Bless You," Roger said.

"No, Skeech. Skeech Ulrich. His father was, ummm, was..."

"Robert," said Bill. "Ulrich. Desert Inn. Vegas."

"Right. Now if I could just think of the name of the show."

Waste Management

Life In An Elevator

TO SOFTEN OR NOT TO SOFTEN

After hearing much more than a daughter should about Mom's irregularity, she decided that a stool softener was in order. The first month of use garnered the desired effect, which was also described in graphic detail. When the bottle emptied, instructions were given to get another at the local drug store since apparently it was helping with all areas of her life, including sleeping well, not needing naps, and improved eye sight.

Two weeks into the second bottle of softeners, it was announced, after another round of unsolicited and unwanted blow-by-blow descriptions, that the pills were now causing insomnia and would no longer be taken. We are now in a non-softener hiatus until further notice.

Life In An Elevator

ONE IF BY PEE

One benefit of living in Arizona, and in particular Sun City, is the abundance of fresh citrus from thousands of orange, grapefruit, lemon, lime, tangerine and tangelo trees. If you don't have a tree in your yard, odds are your neighbors have at least one if not a half a dozen.

Across the street, our snowbird neighbor has two grapefruit, an orange and a tangelo tree in the backyard. They not only let us pick whatever we'd like, they beg us to since they're only in-residence from November until April. So we are fortunate that, starting around Christmas and into May, we get to have fresh grapefruit in the morning and fresh squeezed orange juice whenever we want.

One morning in early April, as I began toasting bagels for Bill and myself, I asked Mom if she'd like grapefruit. She usually has a half most mornings, unless I'm late in asking and she's well into her banana and breakfast bar ritual. This particular morning, however, she declined - apparently forever. "I really think drinking my orange juice and eating grapefruit is making my urine dark."

This phenomenon has been on-going and the source of several conversations - all of which fall into the "Too Much Information" category. And explaining that it's the 10 zillion IU's of vitamin C and vitamin B pills that she takes each day that is causing the bright yellow pee is simply *not* an acceptable explanation. It always garners a "Hmmmmf" response, with the 'I hear you but don't believe it because you're not a doctor or a vitamin professional' inflection.

Two weeks later, I was privy to another update on the ever-perplexing colored pee report.

"I'm going to stop taking my B-12 and B-Complex vitamins" Mom announced.

"Oh?" I asked, knowing *exactly* where this was going.

"Yup. I haven't taken any for a couple of days and when I go to the bathroom it's a normal color. I really think it was the pills."

"You think so?" I responded.

"Yes, I do. So I'll be eating grapefruit again, too."

Life In An Elevator

THE SOFTENING SAGA - PART 2

Just when I thought the waste management reports were over, Mom had a new update. Three weeks after she stopped taking her stool softeners because she thought they were causing insomnia, she decided that she might have been wrong. Instructions were given for a drug store run.

"Be sure to get the same brand that I took the first time," she instructed.

"Which brand is that, Mom?" I asked.

"I don't remember but you'll know it when you see it," she responded.

"How will I know it? I didn't take them, you did."

"Because there's a picture of the pills on the box and it'll say 'Stool Softener' on the label."

"But don't they all say that on the label?"

"No, some of them say something different. So be sure not to buy one of those."

"What's different?"

"It doesn't look the same. You'll see."

"OK Mom. That's clear as mud."

"No it's not."

"Not what?"

"Mud. I think they're white."

Life In An Elevator

MEXICAN BEANS

We were eating taco salad the other night - except for Bill. Taco salad is a girly thing, so he was eating burritos, which is much more manly. As Mom and I made our way through the taco meat, cheese, tomatoes, black olives, green onions, and lettuce to the bottom of the tortilla bowl, she offered up a culinary comment.

"You know, the right way to make a taco salad is to put the Mexican beans on the bottom, not on the top."

"Oh," replied Bill, who is the resident chef. "And why is that?"

"Because that's how they're made."

"How they're made where?" he persisted.

"In restaurants. And probably in Mexico. It's common knowledge. In fact when I used to eat at the club, I had to tell the waitress about it so they'd get it right."

"I see," he said. "So that particular restaurant had it wrong?"

"Yes, they did. But it's understandable because it's not a real restaurant, just part of the club house for the golf course. A real restaurant puts the beans on the bottom."

"Mom, what difference does it make if the refried beans are on the top or bottom?" I asked.

"Because, if they're on the bottom they mix in with the lettuce so you get better roughage, which is really important when you get to be my age, if you know what I mean."

I looked at Bill and silently shook my head, praying he would not take the bait. Unfortunately, Mom had him at 'Because' and he was hooked.

"No, what do you mean?" he asked. "I thought roughage was good at any age."

"Well I suppose so, but when you get older, things get harder and so roughage is good. But stool softeners are better. So I guess a combination of lettuce, Mexican beans and stool softener is a perfect meal!" she said with a giggle as she snapped off a piece of taco shell and popped it into her mouth.

Bill looked dismally at his half-eaten burrito, then up at me, his appetite obviously gone. I looked back at him with a smile and shrugged an 'I warned you not to ask' as I dug into the delectable roughage in my tortilla bowl, visions of future bathroom bliss dancing through my head.

Life In An Elevator

THE SOFTENING SAGA - PART 3

I was smearing peanut butter on my egg bagel one July morning when the silence was broken by a poop update. I'm not sure what prompted this because the last thing Mom and I were talking about was why our snowbird neighbor Fletch's wife doesn't want to live here all year long. "Maybe because it's going to be 112 today?" I asked.

"Maybe. Oh, you know" she announced after a 10 second pause. "Ever since I've been taking those stool softeners, my BM's have been perfect."

I stopped, my peanut butter-laden knife poised centimeters above my golden, toasty bagel, thinking maybe if I didn't respond, she'd move on to another totally unrelated subject. Wrong.

"I used to just push and strain and all that would come out was a little ball, like this," she said, forming a malted-milk ball sized circle with her thumb and forefinger.

So now I have peanut butter oozing onto the kitchen counter and visions of my mother pooping Whoppers and Milk Duds.

"You know," she continued. "When I was pregnant with you, it was so bad that I actually popped a... ummm, you know, a thingy.

I knew I shouldn't respond. I knew I could remain silent and it would go away... but, I couldn't help myself. "Hernia?" I asked. "Hemorrhoid?"

"That's it. The second one. I popped a hemorrhoid. I still have it, I think."

"Well, Mom," I said with what I hoped was finality in my tone. "I'm glad they help."

"They really do. Did you know that Frank got a new roof?"

And so it goes - I just love these mother and daughter chats.

Life In An Elevator

Friends and Family

Life In An Elevator

LIFE LESSON #19

Our grand kids came to visit this weekend. Amber is 9 going on 16 and Jack is 6. Amber is a typical girly girl - hair-do re-dos, surfing the internet for cloths and accessories, and dreaming of being a singer - then acting it out every time she goes into the bathroom. She's not American Idol material yet, but that doesn't stop her from belting out a Bieber song or something from a Nickelodeon show.

Jack, on the other hand, likes to play with our PS3. Or, when we cut him off after he's played for an hour, he likes to use Bill's computer to listen to music or play kids games. And he likes to talk. And talk, and talk. And he's also quite the philosopher.

For example, when we took the kids to the pool for the afternoon, Bill plopped down on the edge of the deep end and dangled his feet in the water while he watch the kids play. After Jack jumped into the water, trying to create the biggest splash possible, he swam up to Bill, grabbed his feet like they were ladder rungs, and said "You know, Papa, here's a life lesson. Don't ever do a cannon ball into a Jacuzzi."

Yes, Jack says things like 'life lesson.'

Life In An Elevator

DON'T YOU JUST HATE THOSE X-RATED CONDOS?

Bill and I were helping our 88 year-old friend Vivian Rose with a garage sale in preparation for her move into an assisted living community. During a lull in the sales activity we were sitting around talking about the weather, politics and other random topics while waiting for the next car to pull up and, hopefully, buy everything we had left so we could get out of the heat. We had just finished discussing hurricane Irene and mulling over the Republican field for the upcoming 2012 election when Vivian made another U-turn in the conversation.

"You know, it's a shame the way kids are being raised now a-days," she said.

"How do you mean," asked Bill.

"Well, they spend all their time texting and not enough time talking."

"I know," I offered. "Plus they aren't allowed to 'lose' at anything. Everyone has to win. They're in for a rude awakening when they get out into the real world."

"And the worst thing is," Vivian interjected. "They're teaching 8th graders how to use condominiums! I think it's just disgraceful," she huffed.

Life In An Elevator

TAKE MY MONEY, PLEASE

We were having some yard work done by Mr. Gonzales, a long-time local landscaper. After several days of trimming, chopping and hauling, we asked if he could cut back some of the 50-year old cactus that was infringing into the neighbor's yard. Since Mom had been complaining about this for months, she offered to pay the modest $145 he was charging. Once the work was complete, we asked her to write him a check.

"No, you pay him and I'll pay you back."

"But why?" I asked, knowing full well the answer.

"Because, I don't want him to have my checking account number."

"But we've written him half a dozen checks and our account is still intact."

"I don't care. I see the news about how scammers are cheating seniors out of their money and stealing their identity and I'm not comfortable giving him my check."

"Oh... but it's OK for him to have our checking account number? He can steal from us?"

A wrinkled brow and thin-lipped frown answered my question. We wrote the check.

Life In An Elevator

MR. WINKY

My mother thinks two-piece bathing suits are immoral, a movie scene where two adults walk arm-in-arm into a bedroom and close the door will cause teens to have unprotected sex, and has to close two doors before using her bathroom. So, keeping this in mind, I suppose I should feel good about the fact that Mom has become so comfortable with Bill that she thinks of him as a son. And why should I come to this conclusion? Because the other morning when the phone rang, Mom decided to answer it.

I was in the garage doing laundry (yes all you Northerner's, our washer and dryer is in the garage) and Bill was in the shower. Mom plopped the phone on her walker seat, rolled down the hall, and flung open the bathroom door. This wasn't bad enough. She then slid open the shower door and the following exchange occurred.

"You have a phone call" she stated manner-of-factly, trying to hand my soaking husband the phone.

"What the h***, can't you see I'm in the shower...and NAKED!!" Bill shouted.

"Well, if you don't want to talk to them, what should I say?" she asked still holding up the phone while the caller was free to hear the exchange.

"How about the truth? I'm in the shower and I'll call back?" says hubby, desperately trying to hide Mr. Winkie.

"OK", she answered, speaking into the receiver "He's in the shower and will call you back".

"Thanks for passing that along" Bill said sarcastically. "Who was it?" he asked as she hung up and headed out of the bathroom.

"I don't know" Mom replied. "I think I forgot to ask. If it's important, I guess they'll call back."

"Or put the whole thing on U-Tube!" Bill shouted after her as she made her way down the hall.

"Nope," she yelled back. "I don't think that was their name."

77

Life In An Elevator

BITE ME?

Our grand-daughter Amber was turning 9 in a week. While spending the weekend with us, Bill wandered into our home office where she was logged onto a website where she could pick an avatar and changes its hairstyle and clothes and play games to earn points to get different hairstyles and clothes.

"What are you doing kiddo?" he asked coming up behind her.

"Well, Papa, I'm on Friv just doing stuff. But I need to talk to you about something."

"Oh? Well what's up?"

She swiveled around in the chair and, with a very serious look on her face, she reached for Bill's hand. "Papa," she started. "As you may or may not know, I have a birthday coming up."

"Yes, I know. It's August 17th."

"That's right. And I've developed an interest lately in vampires."

"Really. Vampires," he responded, trying to look serious.

"Yes. And so for my birthday, I'd like you to think about getting me some vampire teeth."

Bill smiled, thinking of the white and red wax teeth of our youth. "Well, maybe. I'll have to think about it."

As quickly as a seasoned hacker, she spun around to face the keyboard, clicked on the Explorer icon and typed in a Web address. Lo and behold, up popped VampireFangs.com with a full blown video. These were not your Halloween waxed teeth. These were glistening white, pointy sharp retractable fangs that fit in front of your incisors.

"These are the ones I want, Papa," she exclaimed, clicking on the video start button. "They're really cool."

Once Bill regained his power of speech, he responded with remarkable calm. "Well Amber, you may or may now know, but my birthday is three days after yours."

"I know it is," she said, smiling sweetly. "Let's make a pact. I'll get you whatever you want if you get me vampire teeth."

"OK, how about this. I'll get you vampire teeth if you get me a golf cart. It can even be a used one. Because that's what I really want for my birthday."

She seemed to actually think about it for a moment or two before looking up and saying, with all seriousness, "I'll get back to you, Papa."

Life In An Elevator

SINK OR SWIM

Bill and I took our grand kids, Amber and Jack, to the children's pool on a 110-plus Sunday in August. They enjoy it because there's a deep end, which is contained within the small angle of the L-shaped pool and the kids were allowed to jump and dive from the edge. No running, no skipping, no rough-housing, no slide, no noodles, but when we signed in the receptionist gave us a couple of diving rings so the kids could swim to the bottom of the 9 foot depth and retrieve them. This is a great plan unless your 6-year old grandson can't get to the bottom because he bobs up like a life preserver whenever he attempts to go more than 12 inches below the surface. And that's when Jack met Craig.

Craig was two or three years older than Jack, he was refreshingly polite, and he never, *ever* stopped talking. As he paddled across the deep end of the pool towards us he was talking, he continued chattering as he hung off the ladder, went up the ladder, and proceeded to do a cannonball back into the pool.

"I think this type of dive was invented in Hawaii," he babbled, preparing to jump into the water. "That's because I saw these divers going off cliffs when I was a little kid and I went there with my mom and..." At this point he shut up as he made direct contact with the water and disappeared momentarily. I can only assume that he stopped talking once his head went under the water. Or not. Maybe he continued blathering away while he was submerged because his one-man dialogue seemed to pick up in mid-sentence as soon as he surfaced.

"And so, if you just tuck your legs in, it's a proven scientific fact, it'll make a much more impressive splash," Craig continued his litany, switching from diving techniques to favorite vacation spots. "Although," he said, paddling over to Bill, who was sitting on the pool's edge, and reaching for his foot from which to hang, "I found Florida to be more entertaining than Hawaii. But then again, California's pretty exciting. There's lots to do there, even if you're on a budget, which my mom and dad never are. I also like..."

Hanging from the ladder, which was right next to Bill, Jack looked from me to his grandpa and back again before finally addressing Craig for the first time since he invaded our space. "Hey dude, you can do that somewhere else."

Un-phased, Craig looked at Jack and said "You know, if you want to learn how to touch bottom I can teach you. I learned how when I was a lot younger than you. In fact I learned how to do that before I could even swim, which I learned how to do when I was really little, like maybe 3 or 4."

I looked at Jack and said "I think he wants to be friends, Jack. Maybe you should ask him his name."

"Hey dude," Jack said, wedging himself between his grandpa's foot and Craig. "what's your name?"

Life In An Elevator

"Craig," he answered. "I'm from Minnesota and we're visiting my grandma. That's my mom and dad over there," he said, pointing at a couple on the far side of the pool. When we all turned our heads and looked in their direction, I think they actually tried to duck under water. Maybe they were hoping we'd continue to entertain their chatty son so they'd catch a little break. Or maybe they were making bets on how long it would take until Craig drove us screaming from the pool. Or maybe they just enjoyed blowing bubbles at each other under the cool, calm surface of the pool. It didn't matter, because they made no attempt to corral him down to their end of the pool and Craig just kept on talking.

As I tread water in the corner of the deep end, Jack paddled up to me and put his hands on my shoulders. He looked at me with his big brown eyes and whispered "Nana, we've gotta get the heck out of here. He's driving me crazy."

"Yeah," chimed in Amber. "He won't shut up."

"Well, OK," I said, looking at Bill, who nodded his agreement. "If you're both ready to go, we can make our escape."

"Cool," said Jack. "Just give me a minute."

He turned to Craig and interrupted his diatribe on his soccer skills. "Hey, dude, how long can you stay under water?" asked Jack.

"Oh, quite awhile," said Craig. "Maybe two or three minutes. My record is four, but that was in salt water where you can stay under longer."

"OK then," Jack countered. "Race!" And under he went.

"Oh, well then, just let me take a deep breath. You know," he continued, in between deep inhalations. "I won't go as long because I haven't had a chance to really get ready." And with that he held his nose and popped below the surface.

As soon as he did, Jack shot up like a torpedo exiting a submarine, grabbed the ladder and scurried onto the cool decking where we were gathered with our beach bags and towels like refugees escaping a tyrannical government.

"Run!" Jack yelled.

"No running," Bill and I said together.

"Then walk really, really fast!" Amber shouted, heading toward the exit.

As we made our escape, I glanced across the water at Craig's mother and father. She gave me a feeble wave and his dad just shrugged. In the distance, we could hear splashing and Craig shouting "A new record! That was at least five min... hey, where'd you guys go?"

Life In An Elevator

I'm Just Saying

Life In An Elevator

MOM-ISIMS

We all have what I call "isims." You know, those quirky, endearing words and phrases you use to explain or describe or inquire. Mom has her own set of mom-isims. Some of her favorites are thingy, who's it's, do-hickey and whatchamacallit. She generously peppers her daily conversations with mom-isims, substituting actual words and phrases at random and with no apparent sense of logic. The scary part is, I usually know what she's talking about.

We were watching the local weather one morning and, while I was pouring myself another cup of coffee, Mom said "They said who's it's is having a, you know, a thingy about going."

I stopped in mid-pour and, as my brain attempted to turn backwards in my skull, I blurted out "Wiener is having a press conference to announce his resignation?"

"Yes, that's what I just said," she replied, calmly turning to the obit section of the newspaper.

I really scare myself the way I know what the heck she's talking about. Bill isn't scared of me, just in awe.

Life In An Elevator

I'LL TAKE THINGY'S FOR $20, ALEX...

Gazing out the dining room window into the backyard, Mom turned to Bill, who was six feet away in the kitchen trying to pound a chicken breast into an 16 inch pancake for schnitzel, and asked "What's that?"

Too late he responded, "What's what?" then realized he was going to be a contestant on the dinner-time game show *Guess What I Mean*.

"That thing over there?"

"Over where?"

"There, in back by the who's its"

"What who's its?"

"You know, the thingy on top of the whatchamacallit."

"Mom," he said with a sigh, as he turned to face her, meat mallet in hand. "What thingy on which whatchamacallit are you talking about."

She pointed her somewhat palsied finger towards the backyard in the general direction of the patio. "Right there. That thingy."

"Do you mean the cactus garden on the table?"

"No, the thing next to it."

"The solar light?" he asked, hopefully.

"Is that what that is? Does it light up?"

"Yes, once it's dark," then mumbled quietly, "isn't that what lights do?"

"Oh, I wondered because I've never seen it before."

"It's been there ever since we had Lupe lay the patio - about nine months ago. You've asked me at least half a dozen times before what it was"

"I mean I've never seen it lit up," she replied.

"That's because you make us put the blinds down at dinner time," he responded. "And it's still light outside."

"Well, I don't want people watching me eat."

"I thought everyone else in Sun City was eating dinner then too," he commented, preparing to attack the chicken once again with the meat mallet.

"Oh, no. Most of them are already done. We eat pretty late now that you guys are here."

"Really?" he said. "Six-o'clock is late? Well aren't we cosmopolitan."

Life In An Elevator

Bill continued to pound the chicken with renewed vigor, grumbling to himself "all she had to do was ask, what's that round thing by the cactus on the patio table." The schnitzel was exceptionally thin that night.

Life In An Elevator

DINING OUT MEANS EATING IN

After eating dinner at a local Italian restaurant, Bill commented on the pleasant patio eating area as we were walking back to the car.

"It's nice out here, we should have eaten al fresco." Bill said.

"Al who?" Mom asked.

"Outside," Bill answered.

"He's outside?" she said, whipping her head around.

"Not 'he,' Mom," I said. "Al fresco means eating outdoors."

"I don't like eating outside." Mom replied.

"Why not?"

"Because I never have." she said.

"Well, why not try it?" he asked.

"I don't know, but I don't think I'd like it."

"Why not," Bill persisted.

"Because its outside!"

Life In An Elevator

BRIGHT LIGHTS AND OTHER NIGHT TIME FUN

Mom walked into the kitchen the other morning and asked Bill, "When you got up at five o'clock did you see the bright light?"

"No" he replied, wondering if this was going to be a repeat of last spring's bright light sighting, which turned into a weeklong saga. It went something like "I saw a bright light, did you?" Followed by "look out there, can you see the bright light?" and then final update that concluded with "it turned out that I was looking a street light without my glasses."

"Well, I got up around one in the morning and there was a bright light outside my window" she began

"You didn't go towards it, did you?" Bill, quipped.

"No, I didn't go outside," she replied, not getting the humor in Bill's remark. "I just raised my blinds, but I still couldn't see where it was coming from," she continued.

"That's good. We're not ready to lose you," Bill replied, trying another stab at joking around.

"So then I went into my bathroom and looked out the window, but I couldn't see anything" Mom said, ignoring him

"Maybe that's because with window is frosted, " I offered.

Un-phased, she continued with the saga. "So then I went into the hall and into the office and looked out that window, but I still couldn't see anything" she went on, seemingly determined to make this a one way conversation, until she had a 'squirrel' moment. "Boy you know you guys really snore a lot. You should have something done about that. It's not as bad as Patty's father used to snore, but it's not good."

...and that's another "Bright Light" saga de-railed, but replaced by the knowledge that my 85 year old mother is wandering around the house at one o'clock in the morning evaluating our sleeping habits.

The next night on the 10:00 news, there was a story about a couple of women in Chandler who saw 'strange, bright lights moving around in the sky.' Apparently, the lights couldn't be explained as yet, so maybe Mom was onto something. Another "Phoenix Lights" legend in the making perhaps? UFO's really seem to love the Valley of the Sun. Could be they're from Venus or Mercury and our summer climate reminds them of home.

Life In An Elevator

OLD COWBOYS NEVER DIE - THEY JUST GET DE-RANGED

We were watching a piece about rodeo's on a morning news program this week. The featured rodeo was in Montana and it was more akin to mud wrestling since the event was held in a downpour. Mom's comments were peppered with "Yuk," "Oh my gosh, what a mess," "Good Grief," and various combinations, including "Good grief, what a mess," Oh my gosh, what a yukky mess," "Oh good gosh grief" and so on.

During what was obviously a carnage of mud, slime and filthy cowboys, she commented "You know, I think when Arizona started out they had cowboys here."

"Well, this is the West, Mom," I commented back.

"I know, but I think there were quite a few of them here."

"You think?"

"Yes, I do, at least before all the easterners moved in."

Life In An Elevator

SKATING ON THIN ICE

During the pre-Olympic skating trials Mom shouted from the living room "Patty, come here, come here and look at this. I've never seen a more feminine outfit on a man before. Look at him. He looks ridiculous."

"Mom, he's a figure skater. That's his costume. Besides, maybe he's gay."

"Well maybe. But if he isn't he should be."

Life In An Elevator

WHAT?!?

Talks with Mom during dinner are usually triggered by something that is reported on the news. The conversations are widely varied, often baffling and frequently hysterical. One night, Bill and Mom had the following dialog...

Bill: "The Diamondbacks seem to have turned around and started to win!"

Mom: "What?"

Bill: (*loud*) "The Diamondbacks have started winning."

Mom: "Who"

Bill: (*louder*) "The Diamondbacks."

Mom: "I know why I can't hear you."

Bill: (*shouting*) "Because I'm sitting on the same side as your bad ear?"

Mom: "What?"

Bill: (*sigh*) "I think it's supposed to be hot tomorrow."

Mom: "Looks like it's supposed to be over 100 tomorrow!"

Life In An Elevator

THE END OF THE WORLD

It was the eve of May 21st, 2011, the end of the world as predicted by some crazy Baptist preacher. On the way to bed, Mom poked her head into the Arizona Room where Bill and I were watching TV.

"I just wanted to let you know that there's going to be news on the news about how history shows why the world hasn't ended yet, which means it probably won't end tomorrow either."

You can't imagine our relief.

Life In An Elevator

MYSTERY CHUNK

This morning, as Bill was putting together chicken salad to have for dinner, Mom came into the kitchen.

"What are you making" she inquired.

"Chicken salad" he replied.

She then patted the package labeled Rotisserie Chicken and, smiling sweetly, asked "What's this chunk?"

Looking at her with a baffled expression, he responded "The chicken!"

Life In An Elevator

THE SAMSON EFFECT

While eating a pleasant dinner of Bill's most excellent chicken schnitzel, a back-to-college commercial came on that featured a cute blond with Alice in Wonderland hair who was obviously enchanted with her newly decorated dorm room thanks to the wonderful selection and prices available from Target. Suddenly, Mom got a serious look on her face and asked "I wonder if that girl's going to have problems later in life because of her long hair."

Bill and I looked across the room at each other and with the up-lift of his eyebrows and the rolling of his eyes, he signaled "you take this one because I'm not touching it!"

I figured I'd bite. "What do you mean problems?"

"You know," she said. "Problems with her strength."

I tried to choke back a laugh, but it didn't work as well as I hoped because the applesauce I was eating came out my nose. This, in turned cause Bill to almost gag on a green bean. Mom, on the other hand seemed oblivious to the fact that food was spurting from parts of our face - none of which was our mouth.

"It's a known fact that having long hair can drain you of strength."

Wiping applesauce from my upper lip, I asked "Known by who?"

Bill chimed in, "Samson maybe?"

"Well, there's that. But it's a scientific fact. Hair's alive and the longer it grows the harder it is on your body."

"Mom, women have had long hair forever. Look at the movie stars when you were young."

"They all had short hair."

"No they did not. What about Veronica Lake and Rita Hayworth?"

"Short hair."

"Jane Russell? Kathryn Hepburn?"

"Short."

'What movies did this woman watch?' I asked myself.
"OK, you win. I'm going to go cut my hair now so I'll have the strength to clean up the dinner dishes and get your ice cream."

"Very funny," she responded. "It isn't that long yet. But in a couple of months you'd better think about a hair appointment."

Life In An Elevator

CHINESE TACOS

Mom tends to mangle and confuse words and phrases. For example, Bill made orange chicken and egg rolls for dinner the other night. As the meal was winding down, she turned to Bill and asked "Do you want my taco?"

"Taco?" he asked, looking confused.

"Mom, do you mean egg roll?" I asked.

"Okay," she replied, holding up the egg roll and wiggling it back and forth. "This thingy."

"Oh," I said. "You mean the *Chinese* taco."

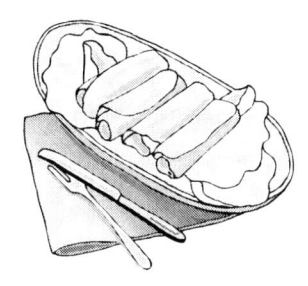

Life In An Elevator

HOW TO BE ARTLESS IN ARIZONA

Bill was online trying to figure out how to increase my blog viewership. During his hunt, he came across a blog entitled "The Art of Procrastination."

"That's what we need to do" I said, peeking over his shoulder at the monitor.

"What? " he asked.

"Learn the art of procrastinating," I replied.

"We don't have to procrastinate," he responded. "There's no reason anymore because we're retired so we don't have to pretend there's something for us to do."

"Well, maybe we need to learn the art of appearing to have something important to do so people won't think we're just the lazy slugs we really are."

"Maybe," he countered. "Or maybe we just need to learn the art of acting like we're procrastinating so it seems like we have important stuff to do but we're putting off doing it because the stuff we're doing at the moment is more important than the stuff we're putting off doing."

I stared at him for a few seconds while he smiled at his own insight. "Honey, you've got way too much time on your hands," I finally said.

"I know," he said. "It's probably because I keep procrastinating!"

Life In An Elevator

DOGGONE

The cover of the Sunday Parade magazine featured a picture of a Jack Russell terrier. Mom, who was finishing up her breakfast, pointed to the picture.

"I had a dog just like that when I was growing up except it was black and white, not brown and white."

"So you had a Jack Russell?" I asked.

"Maybe, but back then they were called Toy Fox Terriers."

"Mom, I think they still are."

"No, I think they changed the name to Jack Russell."

"Why would they do that. They're two different breeds."

"I don't know. Maybe so people wouldn't mix them up?"

Life In An Elevator

ALERT THE MEDIA

Like many elderly people, Mom struggles with her balance. The walker she uses certainly helps, but she still has, what she calls, her 'tipsy' days when her balance isn't as good. These are the days she careens off walls and doorways as she makes her way through the house. Because of this, Mom has gotten into the habit of telling us whenever she's going get dressed each morning or when she takes a shower. We figure she does this so that if she doesn't reappear within an hour or two, we'll check on her to see if she's fallen down. What she fails to recognize is that first, because her entire day is spent on the couch in front of the TV, if she wasn't there for any period of time, we'd become concerned and go looking for her. And second, when she does take the occasional spill, it usually sounds like a sonic boom. She fell in the tub once and I thought the house had been hit by a small plane.

This is why, the other day while I was away babysitting, Bill was confronted with a new announcement. She came into the kitchen where Bill was taking inventory of ingredients for dinner and announced to him, "I'm dressed now." This left Bill somewhat confused because he hadn't gotten the initial "I'm getting dressed now" warning.

"Okay," he responded, while she stood there, waiting for... well, he wasn't quite sure what. "Congratulations?" he asked.

She continued, unphased. "Just thought I'd let you know."

"Okey dokey," he mumbled. "I'll alert the media."

"That would be nice," she responded, turning to leave the room. "I need that. And pick up some M&Ms for me too when you go."

Life In An Elevator

CURFEW

Okay, so it isn't bad enough that Bill and I have lost our jobs, are apparently too old to be hired by anyone else, have lost our home, declared bankruptcy and are now living with my 86-year old mother. No, this isn't humiliating enough. Now we have to put up with being grilled before we go out, after we come home, and the possibility of facing a curfew. Bill is so frustrated by this, he's living vicariously through his new deodorant, which touts a scent of palm trees, fresh air and freedom.

Whenever we leave the house we have to answer the question that is the bane of teen-agers everywhere: "Where are you going?" And when we get home, we have to answer the same question in reverse because Mom forgets what we told her when we left. And we don't dare stay out past ten o'clock. We tried it once. We went out to dinner and our annual movie excursion and didn't get home until 10:20. Mom was waiting up for us.

"Where have you two been?" she asked in a somewhat accusatory tone. "Do you know how late it is?"

"We went to dinner and a movie, Mom," I said. "And it's only a little after ten."

"Well, I was worried about you and I couldn't go to bed. Maybe you should go to earlier movies from now on," she suggested.

"Considering we only go to the movies once a year, we'll keep that in mind," Bill grumbled.

She snorted once and toddled down the hall to bed, flicking all the lights off as she went. Bill and I stood in the dark, looking in the general direction of each other and he asked, "Does this mean we have a curfew?"

"I suppose so, honey," I replied. I guess we'll have to sneak out after she goes to sleep. Maybe she'll think it's just the people who talk outside her bedroom window at two o'clock in the morning."

97

Life In An Elevator

THE RAPUNZEL PHOBIA

This is another episode in the on-going saga of the long hair litany that I wrote about in The Samson Effect. I'm sure I could write in my blog about this particular subject on a regular basis, but I'll try to stop after this one, although I can't promise absolutely since this is a real hot-button for Mom.

"Oh, look," Mom called to me as I was leaving the living room to take her emptied dinner plate into the kitchen. "Vanna's hair is curled."

I rolled my eyes and turned back so that I could dutifully check out Vanna's new do. "Well, that's a nice change," I commented. "Doesn't she usually wear it straight?"

"Yes. And I'm so sick of these women and their long hair!"

For some reason long hair - which starts when the hair gets to be a couple of inches below the shoulders - will periodically illicit this negative, and often vehement response. This frequently repeated complaint is triggered by TV ads, pictures in magazines and newspapers, and now, apparently, by Vanna White.

"Why are you sick of them?" I sighed, knowing what the answer would be.

"Because they all look alike. I just can't tell the difference between them."

"How about some of them are blonde and some are brunette and some are..."

"Doesn't matter. They all look the same. And it's especially bad if their middle aged - like you and me."

"We're middle aged?" I asked rather incredulously.

"Well, you know what I mean. Older women look ridiculous with long hair. If they'd all just cut their hair short and curl it then they'd look different."

"Wouldn't they all look the same - only with short, curly hair?"

"No," she exclaimed emphatically. "You could see their faces better so you could tell who they were and they'd all look different."

I turned and slunk quietly into the kitchen thinking I'd better schedule a hair appointment since my own locks are creeping towards the dreaded "long" stage. After all, I wouldn't want my own mother to be unable to recognize me. That would be a bad thing. Right?

Life In An Elevator

ALERT THE MEDIA

Like many elderly people, Mom struggles with her balance. The walker she uses certainly helps, but she still has, what she calls, her 'tipsy' days when her balance isn't as good. These are the days she careens off walls and doorways as she makes her way through the house. Because of this, Mom has gotten into the habit of telling us whenever she's going get dressed each morning or when she takes a shower. We figure she does this so that if she doesn't reappear within an hour or two, we'll check up to see if she's taken a spill. What she fails to recognize is that when she does fall, it usually sounds like a sonic boom and rattles the house. She fell in the tub once and I thought the house had been hit by a small plane.

This is why, the other day while I was away babysitting, when she came into the kitchen where Bill was taking inventory of ingredients for dinner and announced to him, "I'm dressed now," he was thoroughly confused. He hadn't gotten the initial "I'm getting dressed now" warning.

"Okay," he responded, while she stood there, waiting for... well, he wasn't quite sure what. "Congratulations?" he asked.

She continued, unphased. "Just thought I'd let you know."

"Okey dokey," he mumbled. "I'll alert the media."

"That would be nice," she responded, turning to leave the room. "And pick up some M&Ms for me when you go."

Life In An Elevator

THE REAL SKINNY

<u>Every</u> Thursday, when the fashion section in the newspaper comes out Mom calls me into the kitchen where she eats her breakfast, reads the newspaper and does the crossword puzzles.

"Patty, come here, come here and look at this. The fashions for women are terrible, just terrible. You wouldn't catch me dead in these clothes. They're all too short and show too much. Legs and boobs are hanging out everywhere. And look at these two-piece bathing suits. Nope, I'd never wear anything like that. And who in the world would?"

"Well they've been around a long time"

"I don't think anyone should show that much skin, it's disgusting."

"Well Mom, probably not if you're 85 years old or shaped like an over ripe avocado like I am."

"No, probably not. But even when I was younger, I never would have worn clothes like that."

"You know, I have a picture of you from 1955 in a two piece suit and you looked pretty good."

"Well maybe - I just know I'd never wear anything where my boobs were hardly covered or my butt was hanging out."

"Then I guess you're lucky you don't have to worry about today's fashions."

"I guess so, but somebody should worry about it!"

Life In An Elevator

NO GOATS ALLOWED

I help out my son, Ryan, and daughter-in-law, Jamie, by babysitting our newest grandchild 3 days a week. It's a great job because Olivia is the absolute *perfect* baby. We lived out-of-state when our other grandchildren were babies, so this is a real treat. My son just accepted a new job so his hours are changing from working the graveyard shift to working days. As a result, they need a full time sitter and, since I would still like to enjoy part of my retirement, they're going to hire someone to work three days and I'll fill in the other two. Plus, I get to help Jamie with the interviews since I can't have just anyone taking care of my granddaughter.

I was explaining to Mom that I'd be watching Olivia for six hours a day, two days a week instead of four hours a day, three days a week and Jamie would be getting a nanny.

"Well I don't think that's allowed," she said, munching on her breakfast banana.

"Not allowed?" I asked. "What do you mean, not allowed?" I asked, totally confused.

"They live in the city," she explained. "If they lived in the country - you know, out in the desert someplace, it would be different. But they can't do that in the city."

"Do what?"

"Have a goat. I've heard of chickens, but I think a goat would be too big and it wouldn't be allowed. Neither would a cow."

"Goat? Cow?" I asked, totally confused. "What in the world are you talking about."

"You said they were getting a goat."

"Who, who's getting a goat?" I almost shouted, rethinking my choice of a third cup of coffee.

"Jamie and Ryan," she said, matter-of-factly, switching from the banana to a breakfast granola bar.

"When did I say they were getting a goat, for heaven sakes?"

"Just now. You said you had to help them pick one out. And I said they can't have on in the city."

"A nanny, Mom. Not a nanny goat. A nanny!"

"Oh, that's different. They can have one of those. Just make sure it isn't a pervert nanny like you see on TV."

"I'll do that, Mom. No pervert nannies. I promise."

Life In An Elevator

Neighbors and Other Local Wildlife

Life In An Elevator

ESTATE SALES R US

Here in Sun City, folks don't usually have "garage sales." They're called "Estate Sales" because it means someone either died or went into assisted living and there's a lot more stuff to buy than with an ordinary garage or yard sale. Some people have garage sales but advertise them as estate sales to get the additional traffic, like our neighbors across the street. No one died. They're from Michigan and have used the house strictly as a winter vacation rental for several years. They recently sold the house to friends of theirs from Michigan. Bill goes a little crazy because there are a cluster of homes around ours that are owned by folks from the same area in Muskegon, Michigan. He calls our neighborhood Little Motown and dreams of the day that someone from Pittsburgh moves in so he can have a Steelers buddy.

But, back to the estate sale across the street. Mom is having a great time giving us a blow-by-blow of the activity. It doesn't matter that we've tried to escape to another part of the house, the continuing updates just increase in volume. It's even cut into The Price Is Right time. Every couple of minutes she calls out "Another car just pulled up!" followed by "Someone's leaving now!" This is interspersed with a description - so to speak - of the items customers are carting away.

"Oh, look at that, they just sold some lawn chairs. Did we need those? Is that a toaster oven? Maybe not. Maybe it's that other thing. Patty, you know, that other..."

"A microwave?" I shout from the Arizona Room.

"That's it. And, look, there's some kind of book shelf. Do you guys need that for the office? Maybe you should go over there and see what they've got.. Boy there are sure a lot of *MEN* that go to these garage sales." she exclaimed without taking a breath.

"Mom, we had three garage sales last year to get rid of stuff. We don't need someone else's junk."

"It's not all junk. Some lady in a white van left with boxes and now she's back for more!"

"That was Sue and those are the signs for the sale," I explained.

"Well other people are taking away stuff, except for the ones that aren't leaving with anything. You two should go over there. Some of it looks... Oh, here comes another car."

Bill and I are going to spend the day at the pool - and tomorrow and Sunday. We don't care if we fry up like bacon on the griddle. Anything will be better that listening to the Estate Sale Broadcast station that's taken up residence in the kitchen.

Life In An Elevator

NEIGHBORHOOD WATCH

Bill and I were in our office one Sunday morning and as we looked out the window, we could see our neighbor across the street trimming the hedges that spanned the front of his house.

"I wonder why John's doing that," I commented, watching him trying not to cut the trimmer's electric cord.

"Because he doesn't want to help Sue clean out the garage?" Bill offered.

"Maybe. But weren't his landscape guys there a week or so ago?" I asked.

"They were there on the third," Bill said nonchalantly.

My fingers paused on the keyboard and I slowly turned around in my chair to face him. "You know the *date* his yard guys show up?" I asked somewhat incredulously.

"Yup," he said. "They show up the third of every month. And Wes and Gizella's guys show up on the tenth. My life has devolved into looking out the window at the neighbors and dreaming of killing rabbits."

"Oh my God," I exclaimed. "We have to get you a life!"

"Okay," he sighed, returning his focus on John and his hedge trimmers. "Let me know what you come up with. In the meantime, I'm taking bets on whether or not John cuts the cord in half before he's done trimming. You want in on the action, babe?"

Life In An Elevator

THE ARIZONA HYENA OUTBREAK

Driving Mom to the hair dresser, she commented on a news story the previous evening about the alligator problem in Florida. "You know why they have such a bad problem with crocodiles in Florida, don't you?" she asked.

"You mean alligators?" I responded.

"Yes, I mean alligators. It's because people feed them. That's why they have so many of them."

"Really? I thought it was because they were protected for so long. And what kind of idiot would feed alligators?"

"Well, that's why we have a problem here with hyenas."

"Hyenas? Where?"

"Here, in Sun City. Because people feed the hyenas!"

"Hyenas? Do you mean coyotes?"

"Yes, coyotes. The snow birds feed them!"

"That's crazy. Why would people feed the coyotes?"

"Because they're stupid - and that's why we have so many rabbits... because people feed the coyotes so they don't eat the rabbits."

Life In An Elevator

OMG - JESUS SAW ME NAKED!

Vivian is our elderly neighbor and her backyard adjoins ours. She's a delightful woman of Swiss and German descent. Her cheeks are pink, her face unlined and her age a mystery. One evening at dusk, I was talking to her while she picked some tangerines from one of her many fruit trees. During the course of our conversation, she mentioned that she has a picture of Jesus on her bedroom wall.

"I love my picture of Jesus," she sighed. "But sometimes it's not very convenient to get ready for sleep in the bath."

"Why don't you get ready in your bedroom?' I asked.

"Well, dear, because I can't be naked in front of Jesus."

"Okay" I replied rather dubiously.

"And" she continued. "I have to close the door in the bathroom so Jesus won't see my reflection in the mirror when I'm naked."

"But Vivian," I responded. "Don't you think Jesus knows what you look like naked?"

"Well of course he does dear," she said smiling sweetly. "But that doesn't mean he wants to look!"

Life In An Elevator

TALIBAN RABBITS

Have I mentioned that there's a really bad rabbit problem here in Sun City? Well, there is!

These furry little bundles of cuteness are everywhere and in astounding numbers. And they eat anything... flowers, shrubs, fruit. They eat low-hanging leaves on citrus trees and Mesquite trees. They eat the oranges, grapefruit and lemons that have fallen to the ground. They'll even eat cactus. I've caught them munching on prickle pear paddles, totem poles and red barrels. They eat the spring cactus blossoms, the flowers and the meat of the plant.

But their absolute favorite things to devour are succulents. These are drought-resistant, usually picker-free, moisture-loving little salad bar delights for rabbits. We have a couple of succulent gardens around the house. One is outside the kitchen window and is protected by a decorative wrought iron fence. The other is in the backyard and borders the sun room. This one is surrounded by a chicken wire fence, which worked for a little while until the rabbits discovered they could lift the wire from the bottom enough to allow them to squeeze underneath. So Bill and I reinforced the perimeter with large rocks along the entire fence line, both in front and behind the base. Unfortunately, this hasn't stopped them. Two mornings in a row now, Bill has found one determined little varmint inside the fencing, happily munching on an ice plant.

The first morning I found a small break in the wire along the base where a determined little critter could slip through. So I closed the hole. The next morning, neither Bill nor I could find a breach so I have reached the only possible logical conclusion... a rabbit catapult. Yes dear reader, a Rabbitpult!! This is the only way they could be getting in unless it's a new generation of bunnies that have super powers. In which case, all is lost!!

Life In An Elevator

WILEY COYOTES

Walking into the kitchen this morning, I mentioned to Mom that another coyote had just wandered by.

"That's two this week," I commented.

"It was probably going to the golf course," she said.

"No, it was going in the opposite direction," I said, pointing southeast.

"Well the golf course is over that way."

"No, Mom, that's 91st Avenue. The golf course is the other way," I said, pointing west.

"But the golf course winds around."

"Not towards 91st, Mom."

"Well maybe it was just going to take a different street."

"Maybe," I conceded. "Too bad it didn't stop here for a rabbit or two," I said as I walked out of the kitchen.

"It probably knows where someone is walking a little dog," she called out as her parting shot. "They're easier to catch and that's where it's going."

Life In An Elevator

POINT, CLICK, ARRRRG

There are lots of great benefits to living here in Sun City. They have half-a-dozen recreation centers, each with a pool, spa and workout room. There are tennis courts, Bocce ball courts, shuffleboard courts and one has a Pickleball court, which is a hybrid racket game that combines badminton, tennis and ping pong. It's played on a court with a net similar to a tennis net, a hard paddle and a wiffle ball. There are libraries, mini golf courses, a small lake with boats for rowing and fishing, and a couple of bowling alleys. And the best part - besides all of this being included in the moderate HOA fee - is it has the potential of providing a wealth of blog material.

For example, the other day Bill and I stopped into one of the rec-center libraries to drop off a DVD we'd borrowed. As we waited in line, the octogenarian in front of us was complaining to the librarian about one of several computers that are available for use.

"It won't go where I want it to go," he was yelling. "I keep pointing the thingy and pushing it around, but it won't go where I tell it to go."

"Sir, what exactly is it you're trying to do?" Mrs. Armstrong, the librarian asked.

"I'm trying to send an email to my grandson in Pittsburgh," he said. "But every time I move the whosit's to the place, nothing happens."

"I see," Mrs. Armstrong murmured knowingly. "Did you make sure the pointy thingy was on top of the envelope picture?"

"What antelope picture?"

"No, not antelope, *envelope*."

"What would I need an envelope for. I'm trying to do this on the computer."

"No dear, not a real envelope. You know, an icon."

"I don't know if you can, I only know that I can't!"

"No, no, icon, *icon*. It's a little picture of something."

"I'm not trying to send a picture. I'm having enough trouble trying to send the blasted email."

With this, Bill tapped him on the shoulder and said, "I think I can help you out, sir."

He turned to Bill and replied sharply "I'm not ready to leave yet son, I've got to send this gall danged email first!"

Life In An Elevator

THE TARANTULA IN THE DRYER

I think many people who don't live here are under the impression that scorpions and Gila Monsters and tarantulas run rampant throughout the State. This is mostly not true. Gila Monsters sightings are rare. During the ten years I lived here between 1976 and 86 I only saw one and that was on a long, boring, pre-interstate, mirage-laden drive from Phoenix to Yuma. It was crossing State Route 85 at a leisurely pace. I slammed on the brakes and came to a stop on the right shoulder just as it was entering the desert on the other side of the road. I must admit, I was impressed.

Scorpions are a little more prevalent. But after living in the north Atlanta suburbs of Georgia for over 20 years, scorpion sightings weren't a big shocker. For those of you who don't live near the North Georgia mountains, or new suburbs around Lake Lanier, yes, there are lots and LOTS of scorpions in Georgia. Bill killed an average of one every six weeks or so during the ten years we lived in Flowery Branch. And during the ten years I lived in Phoenix, I only saw two! But that doesn't count the one I found on Bill's bed pillow the week after we moved to Sun Cit. I dumped it - the scorpion, not the pillow - in the toilet and vowed never, ever to tell him about it.

Tarantulas are a different story. You really don't see them much in the heavily populated areas in and around metro-Phoenix area. I saw four at once one time driving north toward Wickenburg on State Route 60. It was dusk and traffic was almost non-existent. They were marching in a line along the edge of the black top, just off the right shoulder of the road. I actually passed them, did a double take in the side mirror, stopped and backed up. I was driving a little RX7 at the time, so it was easy to reach over to the passenger door and open it for a closer view. They were moving past the open doorway when the largest of the four who was taking up the rear, stopped, turned toward me, and reared up on his back legs. Now, I don't know a whole lot about tarantulas except they're big, hairy and they can jump. So I slammed the door closed and sped off, glancing in my rear view mirror to make sure there were still four and the big guy hadn't hitched a ride on my bumper.

Anyway, the point of this story is that after a piece on a local station about a "spider farm" that milks tarantulas and other spiders for venom to create serum, Bill mentioned that he hadn't seen a single scorpion in the almost two years since we'd live here.

"I know," I said, not making eye contact. "It was a lot worse in Georgia."

"And what about tarantulas?" he asked. "Other than the spider farm, I haven't seen a story on the news about them."

Life In An Elevator

"They stay pretty close to the desert, I think," I replied. "And they don't come out until dusk. We could go on a tarantulas hunt one afternoon if you want. I've seen them north of here on the road to Wickenburg."

"Maybe," he said. "I don't know how eager I am to get up close and personal with a tarantula. I'll let you know."

That was a couple of weeks ago. Yesterday Bill swears there was a tarantula in the dryer.

I was folding clothes while Bill offered to transfer the next load from the washer into the dryer. He came running into the bedroom, eyes wide, babbling almost incoherently.

"There's one in the dryer," he gasped. "I saw it. It looked right at me. It was huge. It was hairy. It was ALIVE!"

I looked at him over the pile of towels I'd just folded and tried to settle him down. "What in the world are you talking about? Calm down. Who's alive?"

"The tarantula," he whispered, as though saying it aloud would be an invitation for it to come into the house. "It's in the dryer."

"A tarantula. A real tarantula? In *our* dryer? No way," I said, folding a wash cloth.

"Way!," he shouted.

"Honey, I just got this load out of the dryer and there was no tarantula. I think I might have noticed."

"Come on, I'll show you. Bring a weapon!" And he dashed out of the room. I followed behind and found him into the kitchen where he was frantically pawing through the cooking utensils, looking for a 'weapon.' He settled on the meat tenderizer, handed me a spatula, and made a beeline for the door leading into the garage and our washer and dryer.

He opened the door slowly, searching the floor for signs of movement. The dryer door was open, but it swings towards the doorway, so we couldn't see inside. We made our way into the garage and Bill moved in stealth mode backwards, away from the open dryer door and the pile of damp clothes laying on the floor, continuously glancing around, on guard against anything that might be crawling towards him. As he got into position 5 or 6 feet from the front of the dryer, he whispered suddenly, "Look, there it is."

I was still standing directly behind the open door, so I peeked over the top and looked into the opening at the empty dryer. And there it was, laying placidly in the back of the drum. It was tannish-brown and fuzzy and only had one furry white leg - and looked amazingly like one of Mom's knee-high hose wadded into a ball and resting on a string of lint.

"Oh my God. And I thought you were crazy," I said softly, reaching into the opening. "Come here little guy."

Life In An Elevator

"WHAT ARE YOU DOING?" he yelled, back peddling another 4 feet further away.

"It's okay honey. I promise, it won't bite." And I tossed the clump of hosiery at him.

He screamed like a girl and ran out of the garage, down the drive and into the street, a meat tenderizer in one hand and a spatula in the other.

"Bill, sweetie, I'm sorry," I shouted, picking up the bundle of nylon and un-balling it. "It's just one of Mom's knee-highs." I dangled it in front of my face. "It's harmless, I promise." He stomped back into the garage, yanked the sock from my hand and stormed into the house.

I followed him in, trying very, very hard to stop laughing.

"What was that all about?" Mom asked as I walked through the living room.

"Oh nothing," I said, wiping tears from my cheeks. "Just a tarantula in the dryer."

"Oh, okay," she mutter, refocusing on Jeopardy. "I thought we had company."

Life In An Elevator

NOT WOLVERINES

There was a story on the local Fox channel's morning show about a bobcat and her pups that were spotted in a neighborhood in an affluent community to the east of Phoenix. They story had just ended when Mom came into the Arizona room to say good morning to me and Bill.

"They've had a family of bobcats in someone's backyard in Fountain Hills," I said. "They showed the babies climbing in a tree and the mother on the concrete wall keeping tabs on them."

"Well at least it wasn't, umm, you know... not wolverines," she replied.

"Not wolverines?" I asked.

"Yes, you know, those other ones."

"Cougars?"

"No, no. They're like wolverines but have that colored fur poking out around their eyes. Maybe badgers?"

"Badgers? What does that have to do with bobcats?" Bill interjected.

"Because they can ruin your house."

"Badgers?" he asked again.

"No, like badgers except with the stuff around their eyes."

"You mean raccoons?" I asked.

"YES! Raccoons. They can really tear up your house. Lil and Al had one in their attic back in Michigan" she said as she turned her walker around and left the room "And it made a terrible mess out of things."

Bill looked at me and asked "Do they have raccoons in Phoenix?"

"I don't think so," I answered. "Or badgers or wolverines either. Besides, what the heck does a raccoon in the attic have to do with a bobcat in a tree?"

"Is that a joke?" he asked.

"Sure," I replied. "Why not. How is a raccoon in the attic like a bobcat in a tree? Neither one are wolverines!"

Life In An Elevator

LOVEY DOVEY

On an unusually hot, 110 degree June day, Mom had an interesting observation for Bill.

"Your favorite birds are mating outside the window," she commented to him.

"You mean the doves?" he asked. "I thought mating season was over."

"Apparently not," she responded.

"You'd think they'd realize it's too hot to be doing that kind of stuff," he said, giving me a wink.

"Well that's because they're in the shade," she answered.

Life In An Elevator

BUGS BUNNY MEETS BILLY THE KID

Bill is convinced that the rabbits are winning the landscape war and he really, *really* wants an air gun. He's been checking out Sunday ads, window shopping sporting goods stores, and has gone online almost daily, looking for the perfect weapon. He's checked out rifles, revolvers, pistols, with and without laser sights, semi-automatics, automatics and, probably, air powered bazookas. I'm waiting for the final rabbit attack that will put him over the edge and put a BB gun in his hands.

The latest assault is on an area outside the large picture window of the kitchen breakfast nook. We call it the Kitchen Garden. It's nestled in the corner created by the nook wall and the garage wall and bordered by the walk from the driveway and up to the front door. It's the only shady spot on the property and sports 6-foot by 6-foot garden of pink lady slippers that grow in a profusion of twisty curvy stalks that sprout delicate, tiny pink buds in the summer, three and four foot high agaves, a multi-trunk Madagascar Palm and delicate ground cover. And that's the draw for the rabbits - the ground cover. It's like bunny heroin and they *have* to have it.

Once the garden was finished, it only took about an hour for us to discover that we'd planted a salad bar for rodents, which is why we installed a four-foot high wrought iron fence along the two exposed sides. Things were fine for a month or so until the baby rabbits grew into inquisitive teenagers and discovered they were small enough to squeeze through the two-inch space between the vertical fence posts. So we wrapped chicken wire around the bottom half of the fence, securing it every couple of feet with black plastic cable ties.

This worked very well for a couple more months until the teenagers grew quickly into young adulthood and began systematically pushing against the chicken wire until they'd loosened it enough in one spot to slip through. We probably never would have noticed, and ultimately blamed the plant destruction on insects or birds, had we not discovered one of them escaping the confines of the fence when we drove up the driveway after returning from the grocery store. The sound of the garage door opening must have startled it because it took a flying leap and propelled itself between the 3 inch gap in the upper vertical bars, clearing the chicken wire by at least a foot. It looked like Super Bunny minus the cape; it's front legs stretched forward, it's furry little super-body horizontal to the ground and its fuzzy rear legs straight as rods stretched backward from his fluffy tail. It arced through the fence, cleared the sidewalk, landed gracefully in the yard amid the prickly pear and barrel cactus, and took off like a rocket to its home in the hedgerow across the street.

"That does it," Bill shouted, shaking his fist at the fleeing fur ball. "You #!@&! varmint. You're HISTORY!" And with that, he stormed into the house, forgetting about the melting ice cream and rapidly warming package of

Life In An Elevator

chicken breasts and gallon of milk in the back of the car, and headed for our office and his PC.

I could swear I heard him calling out as he raced down the hall "To the Internet and beyond," but I'm sure it was my imagination.

Life In An Elevator

A SUN CITY ROOFIE

Bill was pouring coffee today when Mom perked up suddenly and commented, "Someone's getting a new roof."

This is a common activity here in Sun City. After all, the community celebrated its 50th anniversary this year. Some of the homes have patch-worked roofs that have never been replace, only repaired over the decades. Most of these are owned by Snowbirds who only live here in the winter or use the house as a rental. Most homes are covered with their second roof, which, at this point, makes them 20 to 25 years old. Mom's roof was replaced about 15 years ago, so we figure we're good for another 5 to 10 years or the next major monsoon - whichever comes first.

Bill glanced out the window and spotted the flatbed truck carrying pallets of shingles. "It's Frank's house," he said, turning back to stirring his coffee.

"Who's Frank?" Mom asked.

"Your neighbor," Bill answered.

"Which one?"

"The one getting the new roof."

"Which house is his?"

"The one at the corner of the cul-du-sac where they've already ripped off half of the old roof!" he almost shouted, sloshing coffee over the cup rim as he furiously stirred it into a whirlpool of caffeine and Splenda.

"He's the one who rides his bike every morning and always wears a funny hat and gardening gloves, right?" Mom asked.

"Yes," Bill cried in relief. "And it looks like he parked his car in Fletch's driveway."

"Who's Fletch?" she asked.

Life In An Elevator

LOOPY

About four years ago, the lady who owns the house next-door came over to let Mom know she was going on a cross-country RV trip with her boyfriend and had no idea when she'd be back. That's when she rented the house to her friend, Mandy. We've had the opportunity to talk to Rita a few times since we've moved here. She's caustic, loud, rude and from New Jersey. Enough said.

She was pulling weeds in the front yard the other morning when our landscape guy Lupe and two of his helpers, drove up to wait for a gravel truck delivery to our house. He was topping our front yard with ten tons of rock, an all-day, back breaking job. Rita wandered over to Bill, who was in the garage getting a cooler of Doctor Pepper ready for Lupe and his crew.

"Is that big guy Loopy?" she asked without bothering to say hello, good morning or how the heck are you.

"Good morning, Rita," Bill said sweetly. "Lupe," he continued, correcting her. "Lupe, not loopy. Loopy means you're crazy."

"Oh, right, whatever," she responded. "Well, when he's done with you, send him over to me." she said, then abruptly walked away.

"I'll be sure to do that," he called after her as Lupe wandered over.

"That's your neighbor who owns the house, isn't it?" he asked.

"Yup," Bill answered as he continued loading Doctor Pepper into the cooler.

"You know, after you referred me to her and we cut down all her fruit trees, she tried to renegotiate the price and pay me less money. I'm never doing any work for her again."

"Can't say as I blame you, buddy. Personally, I think she's kind of loopy!"

Life In An Elevator

THE QUAIL SPA

For Mother's Day this year Bill got me a large clay birdbath and installed it in the backyard, just off the patio. It was ignored for the first couple of days and then the doves discovered it. Doves are just a smaller version of city-dwelling pigeons, except they're probably dumber, if that's possible. They love to sit around the edge of the birdbath, cooing softly and delicately dunking their peaks for a drink. Then they turn around to face out into the yard - a promptly take a dump in the water. By the time Bill cleans out the birdbath each morning, it's as yucky as a port-a-john forgotten at the rodeo grounds for a couple of weeks after the bulls and broncos have left town.

What we noticed as the summer moved as slowly as hot, molten lava toward fall is that a 'pecking' order was gradually instituted and by August, the spa hours had been pretty much established. Around 5:00 in the evening, the smaller birds - sparrows, wrens and finches gather for a drink and chirp fest. About a half an hour later, the medium-sized birds - Doves, Gila Woodpeckers and Killdeer - arrive. The big boys - Grackles, Ravens and an occasional Roadrunner show up next and pretty much scare everyone else away. Then about 6:30 the Quails march in, moving across the yard in groups of four or five or six, and sometimes over a dozen. They hunt and peck in the rocks for bugs, perch around the edge of the birdbath for a drink and a chat, and relax on the patio table and chairs as though it were cool-decking around a pool. I think the sheer number of Quails vends off infringement by any other birds.

The other day, Mom happened to look out the dining room window into the backyard and noticed the Quail gathering.

"Would you look at that," she exclaimed. "I don't think I've ever seen any birds using that birdbath before and now there has to be at least ten of them."

"They use it all the time," I said. "You just never look outside."

"Well, yes I do," she countered. "I look out every morning when I get up."

"Yes, but the Quails don't show up until almost dusk," I explained. "You have to look outside for more than thirty seconds in the morning to see what's going on."

"Maybe," she huffed. "Or maybe there's ants on the patio and that's what's attracted them all of a sudden."

"I told you, they show up every evening."

"Well, sure, since you got ants!" she sputtered, wheeling away to her spot on the couch.

Life In An Elevator

A GRENADE IN THE HAND IS WORTH TWO IN THE CLOSET

I understand that many older folks have years and years and YEARS worth of stuff stored away in their homes. I know this because, after Mom divorced John the Nazi, I spent months cleaning out cabinets, cupboards, and closets because she was going to move in with us and she needed to get rid of several decade's worth of accumulation. For one thing, she had never cleaned out her clothes closet, just moved items from home to home. She had dresses and suits from the sixties and seventies. Some of it was so old it was back in style. Another hurdle was created by her ex, who only seemed to buy in quantity and redundancy. If he needed to replace, oh, say, a door handle, he wouldn't buy one - he'd buy six. If he wanted a new golf shirt, he wouldn't stop at a couple, he'd get a dozen - all the same color and pattern. And don't even get me started on his collection of unopened packages of underwear. He was also an avid golfer and made his own clubs - *scores* of them! Any way, you get the picture. Add to this Mom's compulsion to buy useless junk from Publisher's Clearing House and the Harriet Carter catalog, and you can imagine the garage sale hell I lived in for almost a year. Then, as it turned out, Mom couldn't sell her house, we had to give up ours, and we moved in with her instead.

The reason I bring this up is that, up until yesterday, I thought my mother probably had the weirdest compilation of stuff of anyone living in Sun City. I knew others could come close, just from peeks inside some of the opened garages and undraped windows when Bill and I walk in the neighborhood, as well as visiting the homes of some of our neighbors. Boy was I wrong! As bad as it was cleaning out the clutter, at least I didn't come across any weaponry, like hand grenades, which is what happened to a family cleaning out their deceased father's house a couple of miles from here. The headline in the Sun City paper proclaimed "Live Grenades Found In Man's Home." This guy was a WWII vet and, not only did he have live hand grenades laying around his house, the Bomb Squad - yes, they had to call the Bomb Squad - also found other "live ordinance," whatever the heck that is!

Sorry Mom, I'll never complain about your tweed jumper or ceramic duck collection again!

Out and About

Life In An Elevator

IN THE BAG

I was in the Albertson's checkout line here in Sun City watching Roger carefully put my purchase into my cloth shopping bags. I do try to do my bit and recycle and use cloth bags and I'm pretty good about it. I figure I remember to get the bags out of the back of my car at least half the time - the other half I'm having an adult moment or so busy dodging seniors driving haphazardly around the parking lot that it just slips my mind.

Roger, who is my favorite bagger, is retired and working at Albertson's to supplement his fixed income. Plus he really seems to enjoy himself. He's constantly joking with customers and cutting up with whichever cashier he's bagging for.

I had finished paying and was waiting for Roger to put the remaining items into my third cloth bag when he said, "sorry for the delay. This bag just isn't cooperating today."

"I know," I comment. "They're kind of floppy."

"Yup," he responded. "Pretty much like the rest of us at our age!"

Life In An Elevator

A YARN ABOUT YARN

Taking Mom to run errands is an adventure. Besides going for a bi-annual doctor's appointment or the quarterly hairdresser visit, errands usually entail going to the bank to cash a check, going to the drug store to replenish her supply of vitamins and other over-the-counter drugs or to pick up a prescription. And sometimes, if the stars have realigned in anticipation of, oh I don't know... calamity, havoc, humiliation... we get to go retailing. Maybe to the ladies clothing store for new 'pedal pushers,' or the used book store for a couple of paperbacks, or maybe, like yesterday, to the craft store for yarn and afghan patterns.

We made our way through the store, gather together 6 skeins and an afghan magazine, then headed back to the front of the store to check out. I was almost giddy with relief since Mom hadn't destroyed any displays or end-caps or injured any customers by crashing into them with her walker.

Suddenly, she spotted a clerk at an empty counter close to the entrance and exit doors and made a beeline toward her, ignoring the large "Customer Service - Returns and Exchanges' sign above the register. She plowed past an elderly woman who had just entered the store and was approaching the counter with her bag of returns and an assistant manager who was directing yet another customer toward the counter.

Quickly emptying her skeins from the storage area under the walker seat and pulling out her wallet, she flashed the confused clerk a smile. "Hello, dear, I'd like to pay for these."

"This line is for returns, ma'am."

"Oh my, oh dear," Mom whimpered. "I didn't know. I just wanted to pay for these, but I'll move," she continued, reaching for her things on the counter, then stumbling slightly as she let go of the walker handles. She teetered momentarily but managed not to topple over.

"No, no, never mind," the clerk said, becoming alarmed that she might soon have a senior sprawled on the floor. She quickly rang up the 6 skeins of yarn and the magazine, then gently said "Next time, you'll need to get into the line down there," pointing to the cue of 4 or 5 customers waiting in line at the other end of the store.

"I certainly will do that," Mom exclaimed with a sweet smile.

As she was slowly writing a check for her purchases, the clerk asked automatically "Are you on our email list for coupons and specials?"

"Why no," Mom replied as she finished writing the name of the store on the check. "My daughter has email, can it go to her?"

Life In An Elevator

"Sure, just fill this card out and bring it back the next time you come in," the young woman said, handing me a postcard-sized piece of paper full of little tiny boxes in which to write each letter and number.

"Oh, that's all right," Mom said. "Patty, fill that out while I finish writing the check." Since she was only on the first written number on the check line, I figured we had at least another 7 or 8 minutes.

"Sorry about that," I muttered, trying to apologize to the two women waiting patiently with their return items, as I quickly, and messily, filled in the information.

As we finally moved away from the counter towards the door, I commented to Mom, "I guess next time you'll have to wait in line like everyone else."

"Maybe," she replied, as the door closed behind us. "Or maybe sometimes it just pays to be old and act dumb!"

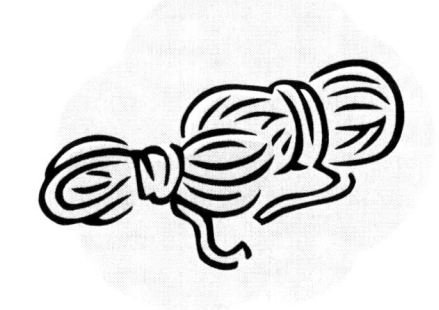

Life In An Elevator

SWIMMING WITH SHARKS

What's more dangerous than swimming with Great Whites? Driving around Sun City! This is on par with maneuvering through an obstacle course peppered with live landmines. First you have to contend with swarms of road mosquitoes in the form of golf carts. Secondly, the vast majority of the cars are heavily armored behemoths like Grand Marquis', Cadillacs and Rivieras because elderly drivers feel protected behind the wheel of their own personal tank. And thirdly, throw in failing eyesight, poor hearing, and nonexistent reaction time, and you get a picture of the adventure to be had driving the streets of Sun City.

Speed limits are mere suggestions meant to warn the senior drivers that meeting or exceeding the posted limit could result in a run-away car. Consequently, most drivers plug along at 5 or 10 mph below the limit. This, however, is in direct contrast to busy intersection behavior. Right Turn Allowed After Stop means just that - stop and then immediately turn right! This rule also applies to turning onto the road from a parking lot exit.

Left turns are approached differently. If the left arrow is lit, it indicates that the left turn must be made very slowly. And getting more than two or three cars through a left turn signal is a rarity. This is because it's another unwritten rule that, when you're cued in the left turn lane, besides proceeding at a snail's pace, you must keep at *least* 4 car lengths between you and the car in front of you at all times. This is a precaution against... oh, I don't know, maybe the trunk popping open and groceries and walkers spilling out or maybe the car in front spontaneously shifting into reverse before it completes the turn.

Turn signals are non-existent. It's bad enough on the residential streets where you're only driving 15 or 20. At least you can break and stop quickly when someone suddenly remembers that that's their house and the driveway is RIGHT THERE. Passing a side street, then quickly stopping and backing up is also apparently allowed.

And then there is the hidden danger of complacency. This happens when you're driving along, no one in front of you, no one behind, and suddenly a car backs down a driveway and, without hesitation, dumps itself into the street and speeds away at a reckless 18 mph. The only except we've found at this point is one lady who lives about a half a mile west of us.

Bill was taking his usual route home from the bank on morning, which winds along on a residential street that has a 25 mph speed limit. He was very happy because there was no one else on the road and he was actually driving a couple of miles per hour over the limit. That's what I love about him, he's such a risk taker. Suddenly, a blue-haired, curly headed woman came speeding up behind him in an older model silver Mercedes convertible. She had on enormous, round sunglasses, a sequined-billed golf visor, and must have been at least 80 years old. She hung on his back bumper, even

Life In An Elevator

when he accelerated to a daring 35 mph. Finally, in a fit of unrestrained impatience she passed him *on the right*, honking and shaking a wrinkled, bony fist at him as she sped by. She hung a left 2 blocks later and disappeared in a cloud of diesel exhaust. As a result, Bill now brakes for fire trucks, ambulances and any silver Mercedes convertible that's more that 10 years old.

Life In An Elevator

PARKING LOT GAMES

The only thing slightly less dangerous than backing out of a parking space in the parking lot of the local Sun City drug or grocery store is trying to pull into a handicapped slot. Unlike most parking lots in an average city or town, handicapped parking is at a premium here. Finding a handicapped spot is like finding a gold nugget in a stream - a rare and exhilarating experience. Part of the fun during a trip to the grocery store is watching 'Musical Handicap Parking,' which is second only to 'Back Out Chicken.'

Musical Handicap Parking is played by two cars, each driven by someone who is at least 81 and has no depth perception. At least a third of the population of Sun City qualifies. Each car must approach the empty parking spot from opposite directions, which means that one of the cars is probably going the wrong way down the lane. The first one to make it into the parking space wins and there are no rules about the vehicle's final parking angle, depth into (or out of) the slot, or its proximity to the cars on either side. The loser is left to continue trolling the rows for another round of play.

Now, as exciting as Musical Handicap Parking sounds, it really can't hold a candle to the thrill of Back Out Chicken. This usually involves two vehicles, but more can - and sometimes do - play. The object of the game is to back out of your parking space without looking, without stopping, and without being bashed in the rear by the car across the row, who is also blindly backing out. The loser is the one who chickens out and stops to allow the other car to complete their exit. Should the cars collide, the winner is determined by 1) who is most oblivious to the impact; 2) who has the fanciest walker; or 3) who has the most comprehensive auto insurance.

Life In An Elevator

RUNAWAY WALKER

I don't know what it is about the digestive systems of the elderly that requires constant conversation but, besides the weather, this is the most frequently discussed topic in Sun City. This observation is based on talks with neighbors, overhearing conversations waiting in line for prescription refills, checkout lane chatter, recreation center and pool side discussions, and last, but not least, Mom's almost daily updates on everything from color to consistency to frequency to volume. I mention this as an explanation for our recent drug store run to replenish Mom's stool softener supply and get more cranberry supplements.

We hadn't been out for awhile so she was a little out of practice steering her walker up and down aisles and maneuvering around people. After finding the vitamin aisle and her cranberry pills, I lost her briefly. She was tottering down the infant and baby supplies row looking for stool softeners when the startled yelp of pain from a Pampers sales rep as she drove over his foot alerted me to her location.

"Mom!" I called to her, waving to get her attention. "Over here, they're along the back wall." She made a beeline toward me, unaware of the sales rep limping away in the opposite direction.

"Did you find them?" she asked, coming to an abrupt stop a millimeter from my left big toe.

"Yup," I answered, pulling a box from the shelf and handing it to her.

"These aren't the right ones," she said without looking at the label.

"Well, they're the same ones I got you last time," I countered.

"No they aren't," she argued. "The last ones came in a bottle, not a box."

I took the box back, opened the top and pulled out the bottle. "Is this what you mean?" I asked.

"Hmmmf," she muttered, taking the bottle and box from me and hanging a right towards the front of the store.

As I followed her past shelves filled with antacids, pain relievers and cough remedies, I grew somewhat alarmed as she continued to pick up speed the closer we got to the checkout counters. She began to weave slightly, nicking an end cap of flip flops as she crossed the center aisle, then picked up speed on the home stretch down the candy aisle. She continued to accelerate as she veered sharply right to avoid a head-on collision with a Pillow Pets display, then had to make a hard left to get in line, which she accomplished on two wheels. She would have made it unscathed if it hadn't been for the man on the scooter who was also waiting in line. Anticipating a rear-end collision in the making, I leapt forward and grabbed her around the waist.

Life In An Elevator

Fortunately, it was enough so that the crash didn't topple the elderly gentleman from his ride, only jarred him slightly.

As I offered an apology, Mom paused for a nanosecond, assessed the wait time, and abruptly veered around the line and plowed toward the second cash register. She stopped quite literally on the heels of the lady who was collecting her change. I apologized again as I quickly grabbed a handle on her walker to bring her to a stop.

"Mom! Slow down." I said a little more loudly than I intended.

"I can't," she responded. "It's running away with me!"

"It can't run away, it isn't a horse. Besides," I reasoned. "It has brakes and no motor. You're pushing it too fast."

"No I'm not," she argued. "Everything goes downhill to the front of the store!"

Life In An Elevator

THE TEQUILA WAGON

One of the major intersections near the house has new car dealers on three of the four corners. And because of this, Bill and I have started our own drinking game. The premise of the game is, every time we take Mom out and have to go through this intersection - which probably occurs 75% of the time - we hold our breath and wait for the inevitable observation, "Boy, there sure are a lot of cars there!" If this comment does NOT happen, when we get home, Bill and I have to down a shot of tequila. So far, we're still on the tequila wagon.

I did have a close call yesterday when I took Mom to her quarterly perm appointment. The only thing she said as we approached the intersection was "Boy, there sure are a lot of lights there," as she noted the array of vapor lights in the Nissan dealer's lot. As we waited at the light she glanced at the Chevrolet dealer's lot on the right, back at the Nissan dealer on the left and finally caddie-corner to the Ford dealer without uttering a sound. The light changed to green, we proceeded through the intersection, past Albertson's, past Blockbuster and past Snuffy's Pizza. I was becoming somewhat concerned that I'd have to throw back an ounce of Jose Cuervo Especial at 10:00 in the morning. And then, just as we were almost past the last car dealer in the area, she came through.

"Boy, there sure are a lot of cars there. That's a Kia dealer you know."

Thanks, Mom, for keeping me off the sauce - at least before 5 o'clock.

Life In An Elevator

THE GREAT STRAWBERRY WAR

Grocery shopping in Sun City is a complex, but elegant dance - similar to the Tango. You steer your cart around as though it were your dance partner, weaving, spinning, and turning deftly and with authority. Because if you show hesitation or - God forbid - fear while navigating the aisles of the local Safeway all is lost. The Great Strawberry Incident of Memorial weekend 2011 is a perfect example.

Bill and I do all the grocery shopping because it's far too dangerous to bring Mom. The last time we did she collided her cart with another in the produce section while jostling for position around the bananas. She also clipped a row of baked beans while careening down the canned goods aisle and ended the trip by taking out an end display of Vanilla Wafers and pudding with a direct hit.

At the end of one shopping excursions, Bill notices a freestanding table with quarts of strawberries marked 2 for $2. Unfortunately, the display was near the front door and we were in the checkout line and didn't want to lose our spot so I offered to go get some while Bill waited in line. As I wound my way over to the strawberries, the crowd got bigger and bigger. I didn't have a cart to maneuver, so I thought it would be easy to sidle up to the display, grab a couple of quarts and get back to the checkout lane with time to spare. Wrong on all counts!

Several feet from the table I was abruptly blocked by two elderly women who managed to 'V' their carts in front of me, parking them blockade-style. When I attempted to move around the barricade, I was side-swiped by a geriatric gentleman in an electric shopping cart. He careened in front of me and made a beeline to an opening at the edge of the display. I decided to veer right and do an end-around, but I almost tripped over a strategically placed cane wielded by a 70-something lady with a determined glare.

Strawberries were being yanked off of the table and shoved into carts at an alarming rate. I knew in that instance that competing against the Sun City weapons arsenal of metal walkers, electric carts and hardwood canes meant no more Mrs. Nice Guy. Shoulders steeled, head down, I bull-dozed my way between a woman on her heavily decaled scooter and another with a metal tri-footed cane, reached fearlessly into the fray and captured my two quarts of berries.

I managed to dash back to Bill just as the last few items were being rung up.

"What took so long?" he asked.

"It's war, honey, war," I answered. "And I won the battle!"

Life In An Elevator

BEACH ANGELS AND STUD MUFFINS

It's been pool weather in Sun City for some time now and Bill and I really enjoy going a couple times a week to cool off. Sun City has 6 different pools of varying sizes, each offering a variety of activities from walking to laps to jazzercise. The people we meet are great and really friendly and, in general, are glad to be enjoying their retirement time here.

But the real reason Bill and I enjoy going to the pools is because we look like younger versions of everyone else there. Bill thinks he looks like a short version of Tom Selleck when in reality he looks more like Mr. Potato Head, and I look like I've swallowed a 50 lb eggplant whole, But the great thing is we both look pretty much like everyone else.

So instead of worrying each spring about losing weight to become "bathing suit" ready, we just order the next size up from the Tractor Supply Company, fill the beach bag with Cheetos, and Bahama Mama's, slather sunscreen on the man boobs and cankles and head to our favorite summertime spot... It's great to fit in.

Life In An Elevator

GOD'S RECEPTION AREA

You know the old saying about Florida - that it's God's waiting room. Well, if that's true, then Laughlin is the reception area to God's waiting room. The entire city is populated with bus loads of seniors from every retirement community in Phoenix, Mesa, Sun City and Tucson. They come in buses, RVs, car pools and mini vans. Clutching their Player's Club cards to their chests, they dash, so to speak, into their casino of choice, knocking over other seniors in their quest to get to their "lucky" slot machine or favorite bingo chair. In a nutshell, the demographics of Laughlin can be described in three words - over sixty-five.

The aisle and paths that wind around banks of slot machines are narrow, and yet walkers, wheelchairs and scooters navigate relatively unscathed like battleships maneuvering through war games. The number of nose tubes and oxygen tanks rival most large city ERs and yet the casino's gaming floors remain one of the last bastions of smoking-friendly establishments in the country. And, unlike Las Vegas, which comes to life after dark, Laughlin nightlife is pretty tame. Venues include former greats like Tony Orlando and Kenny Rogers and Kool and the Gang, as well as a myriad of Elvis impersonators. Casinos offer line dancing or two-step lessons, but most of the guest are asleep by 9:00. They need their rest so they can get up early to wait in line at 6 AM for the $4.99 breakfast buffet.

The first time (and last) time Bill and I went was four years ago when we were visiting Mom and her then husband, John the Nazi. He managed to bully his way to two free rooms, gloating to us on the trip up in the elevator how he *never* pays for a room in Laughlin and damn well shouldn't what with all the money he spends here. We had enough time to dump our bags, open a window to air out the musty smell of old, then do a quick visual survey of our accommodations and conclude the room was worth the price. Minutes later, John the Nazi was pounding on the door so he could give us a brisk walking tour of the hotel, two restaurants, and casino. He then dragged us into the Keno room where he ordered himself a double shrimp cocktail and vodka tonic and proceeded to explain his 'system' to us. Since there is a 10 minute break between each Keno draw, we had to wait for John's results for two separate drawings before he forced us to play a couple of times to make sure we got it right. We managed to escape and found Mom happily playing a poker slot, glad to be free of her overbearing spouse for a couple of hours. After wandering aimlessly and dabbling (and losing) at a couple of slot machines, we planted ourselves at a Blackjack table and dribbled away $30 over the next 3 hours, while taking full advantage of the free drinks.

We spent two fun-filled days and nights and left minus $100 in gambling money, plus a tee shirt that said "Colorado Belle - We're Game If You Are" and vowed never, ever to return. That was four years ago during another life. Yesterday I caught Bill looking online at Laughlin hotels.

Life In An Elevator

"What are you doing?" I exclaimed, looking over his shoulder at the list of hotels.

"I don't know," he said sheepishly. "I just thought maybe we could get away for a couple of days and its closer and cheaper than Vegas."

"Are you crazy? Don't you remember our last trip?"

"I know, but at least the Nazi won't be there."

"Bill, we may be living in a senior community. We may be living in forced retirement. But I will not cave and become one with the Laughlin living dead!"

"Okay, okay, don't get your bun in a tangle, granny."

He'll be out of traction in about a week.